ESSENTIAL READING ON

Leadership

R. ALBERT MOHLER JR.

RANDY STINSON

MICHAEL S. WILDER

TIMOTHY PAUL JONES

JEREMY RHODEN

JEFF ROBINSON

MATTHEW HALL

BRIAN CROFT

THOM S. RAINER

DAVID SILLS

SCOTT CONNELL

RAY RHODES JR.

HERSHAEL YORK

ERIC GEIGER

LARRY PURCELL

NIKKI DANIEL

Contents

01

Leadership and conviction: Recovering the vision

History reveals the role of leadership for great good, and for great evil, but there is no way to remove leaders from the center of the action.

BY R. ALBERT MOHLER JR.

The secular world thinks of leadership as a sociological necessity. Given human nature and the complexity of human society, we need leaders in order to organize human effort into productive channels. History reveals the role of leadership for great good, and for great evil, but there is no way to remove leaders from the center of the action.

In more recent years, leadership has become a secular preoccupation. An entire industry has grown up around leadership, with literally thousands of book titles, countless seminars and personal leadership coaches for hire. Colleges and universities offer leadership degrees and just about every major corporation offers leadership training.

As is often the case, the church has been deeply influenced by this secular conversation. Leadership has become a major focus of evangelical concern, even as it seems that many evangelicals are uncertain about how Christians should think about leadership as a calling and as an art.

Throughout the last century and more, American Christianity has been deeply influenced by the business culture. Early in the 20th century, this was reflected in the emergence of a concern for "efficiency" in ministry, adopting the term that was then at the center of business concern. Later, churches adopted models of organization and management that seemed, oddly enough, to make many churches look like American corporations in terms of structure, culture and even vocabulary. More recently, the concern about leadership has been linked to the large business culture, along with its pragmatism.

In too many cases, Christians have just imported models and concepts of leadership from the secular world. Much of the supposedly "Christian" literature about leadership is just secular thought with a few Bible verses printed alongside. This can lead to the importing of unbiblical models of leadership into the church, and it has produced an evangelical culture of pragmatism that is subversive of both the gospel and of the church itself.

Thankfully, the coming generation of young pastors has generally rejected that model of ministry and leadership. They want nothing to do with the doctrinal minimalism and pragmatism of the secular models and their evangelical counterparts. They have rejected the absence of theology and the marginalization of biblical ecclesiology that has marked so much of the mainstream church culture in the United States.

And yet, as much as I am encouraged by this rising generation's diagnosis of the problem they see, they still have to lead. If the secular world knows that leadership is necessary because of sociological realities, the Christian knows that leadership is necessary because of biblical categories. We are taught in Scripture that God's people require leadership — and urgently so.

In the Old Testament, we read honest accounts of the patriarchs, judges, kings, and prophets who led Israel. In the New Testament, we find the church led by apostles and teachers, who both served and led as the church followed Christ.

The tasks of ministry today require leadership skills that would humble a Fortune 500 CEO. But, even as some of the skills and competencies of leadership are common to all contexts of leadership, the minister of the gospel is called to a very specific form of visible leadership — leadership by conviction.

Conviction — the knowledge of truth that transforms — is the bedrock of Christian leadership. The Christian leader is driven by gospel convictions and a passionate love for the church of the Lord Jesus Christ. The art and science of biblical leadership flow out of the minister's first and foremost arena of leading — and that is the role of teaching.

The minister leads, most importantly, by the faithful teaching and preaching of the Word of God. The New Testament reveals a model of ministerial leadership that is based on biblical convictions and driven by a passion to see Christ's people follow in faithful obedience.

Thus, authentic Christian leadership is deeply doctrinal, inescapably theological, unrelentingly biblical and, by virtue of the Bible's authority, unavoidably practical.

The Christian pastor does not lead by title, or by his own inherent authority. He leads by the preaching and teaching of God's Word. His leadership credibility is established by his exposition of the Bible and by his presentation of biblical truth. He is able to move believers to action, not because he holds an office, but because he fulfills that teaching office with both skill and deep conviction.

Authentic Christian leadership becomes evident when God's people are led to know and to obey deep truths from God's Word when their intuitions and patterns of thought are brought into conformity with the truth, and when believers then go out into the world in faithful obedience to Christ.

And we must never forget that true Christian discipleship is always practical but never merely pragmatic. Thus, the Christian pastor must learn the skills and competencies of effective leadership as an extension of his pulpit ministry, not as a substitute.

The biblical formula is simple to understand and impossible to refute. We live and operate out of our genuine convictions. We do live as we believe. Christians are faithful only when our convictions lead to the right actions, and leadership that rises up from authentic biblical convictions will produce a church that will be taught to live out those convictions in every dimension of life.

In other words, if the church is underled, it is because the church is underfed. Leadership by conviction is the only model of leadership that is worthy of the Christian ministry, and what the church desperately needs in this age is a generation of preachers who are driven by the conviction to lead.

02

What does it look like for a man to lead spiritually in the home and community?

Nine areas for a man to initiate in the home from Ephesians 5

BY RANDY STINSON

Men are to be leaders in their home. It is one of the most critical places for them to lead. That's where leadership all happens. It's where the rubber meets the road. Think about when a man gets married: he immediately doubles the amount of sin in his home. Once you add a couple of kids, it just quadruples. The most critical place for leadership is in the home. Everything — how you lead in the community, how you lead a church — springs from there.

Ephesians 5 gives clear instruction to men and their wives. Here, and in 1 Peter 3 and Colossians 3, it's clear to me that Scripture affirms the man's constant role of leadership, provision, and protection. That leadership needs to be done in a particular way and with particular care. You can't just do it however you want to. God has given men a responsibility, and Scripture shows us what that involves. In this chapter, I will list nine areas where men should initiate in the home. I want to be clear: I don't mean that a wife or a mom can't do any of these. I just mean that, in general, a man ought to be the one more regularly doing these things. If you're not married, it doesn't matter — these are generally applicable leadership principles. But for those who are married, I will take these nine expositional reflections from Ephesians 5 and seek to apply it to practical issues in marriage.

1. VISION

Where are we going?

The leader of anything is the primary keeper of the vision. By vision, I don't mean that somebody went to bed and had a dream. Instead, ask yourself what you want things to look like 10 years from now. What do you want it to be characterized by? What kinds of things do you want to have happen in your home? What should it look like?

One of the greatest vision statements ever made was from John F. Kennedy, who said that before the 1960s were over, the United States would put a man on the moon. Simple as that. Now, he didn't know anything about gravitational pull, rocket propulsion, O-rings, or anything like that. That comes later. The vision was: Within this decade, there's going to be someone on the moon.

Think about this for your personal life. Where do you see yourself in 15 years? Everybody should have some kind of a plan. Hold on to it loosely, because God has a way of changing all of our plans. But have a plan. One of the things my family decided early on was that we knew we wanted to have a lot of children and we knew wanted to adopt. We always had thought we would have a large family. So we made a plan based on that vision. God is sovereign over the picture you have for your life. But you should have a picture. What do you want this thing to look like? That can actually be a fun thing to dream about.

2. DIRECTION

How do we get there?

In this category, we map out some of the details of the vision. You want a strong marriage? Great. Everybody wants a strong marriage — even lost people! Non believers don't go to the altar and think, "I hope this doesn't work out." They hope it works out! Everybody is hoping it works out, or they wouldn't even do it. What most people don't do is put things into place to help them cultivate a strong marriage.

This is where a lot of men fail: They have a lot of ideas, but they won't write down how they're going to do it. You want a strong marriage, then what are you going to do? Write a few things down. My wife and I try to go out on a date night once a week without the kids. That's important. It is important to demonstrate for my children that there is one relationship in the home that's more important than any other: my relationship with my wife. So, I want to have a good marriage, and one way we give direction to that vision is to go out on a date once a week.

You need steps to the plan — you can't just assume it's will just happen. You don't have to have a 100-page document, just write down a little plan.

3. INSTRUCTION

Let me show you how.

Wherever you're leading, because we're fallen, there are going to be obstacles to the plan. You are working by the sweat of your brow, and there are going to be thorns and thistles you are trying to plow. So, I'm not just giving my family the vision and direction and then pulling out and watching them execute it. I'm going to be in there working with them, trying to prepare them for the obstacles that they are trying to face.

4. IMITATION

Watch what I do.

The Apostle Paul said, "Inasmuch as I follow Christ, follow me." That's at the heart of leadership. "Do as I say and not as I do" is failed leadership. It's hypocrisy.

In my family, I model the apology. I show them how to make it right when they mess up, because they're going to do this too. If you can't be the kind of a leader that can model apologizing, then you're going damage the souls of the people you're trying to lead. A lot of men think that if they apologize to their kids, or even their wives, then it's going to make them look weak. Don't ever think that — it's actually the opposite. An apology is powerful. A man as a leader has to be an initiator. He has to be doing it himself.

5. INSPIRATION

Isn't this great?

This is the most fun part in my job as a leader in Southern Seminary and a leader in my home. The leader of anything is responsible for morale. The Southern Baptist Theological Seminary is an incredible place, but it is full of fallen people. It's not a place without problems. It's not a place without conflict. It's not a place without sin. My home is also not a place without conflict, and neither is yours. So when I go home and I say, "This is a great family," that comes from my responsibility to tell them that.

When you think your kids need encouragement, your wife needs it way more. Who better to give it to her than you? That is a beautiful gift you can give your wife. You don't have to bring home jewelry or flowers. Every day you reiterate, "I'm so happy you're my wife, I deeply love you and appreciate you, and I couldn't wait to get home from work today to tell you that." That's free.

6. CONNECTION

You're doing great.

Inspiration is corporate, but affirmation is about the individual. The key to morale is individual affirmation. You have to go to individuals and say, "You're doing a great job." Encouragement is contagious. It becomes part of the grammar of the home. Kind words are like oil in the machine that keeps the gears from grinding.

7. EVALUATION

How are we doing?

This is the burden of leadership. The leader has to pick his head up and look around and say, "Are we doing what we said we're going to do?" Maybe you said you wanted a strong marriage, and you said the way you were going to do that was by going on a date night once a month but you haven't been on a date night in two months. So you evaluate and change course.

8. CORRECTION

Let's make a change.

Simple as that. After evaluation comes correction. It's never too late to do what you said you would do. Some of you men may just have let some things go too long. And you think, "There's no way, there's no way to pull out of this. I'm in too deep." You probably don't, but somebody does. I have been in the ministry for 28 years. I have seen some train wrecks that you would never believe, but God intervened and there was repentance, heart change, and the gospel had its way in their lives.

9. PROTECTION AND PROVISION

I'll take care of you.

This is just the overarching sentiment of leading, and it should be expressed with great humility and full knowledge that you can't really keep harm from happening to your children. I can't stop cancer from coming into my home. I can't stop a drunk driver from running into a member of my family. I'm not saying that nothing bad is ever going to happen to my family. I'm saying, "When it does, I'm going to be here. I'm not leaving you." I've learned over the years to express it as often as I can. I will spend the last drop of energy and love and life taking care of my family, and I can be counted on by God's grace. That's what I try to communicate to them.

This chapter is adapted from a 2014 sermon delivered at Desert Springs Church in Albuquerque, New Mexico.

03

Life as a shepherd leader

What this young man needed wasn't merely an improvement in his people skills — though, frankly, he could have used that too. What he needed was to understand the difference between cattle and sheep.

BY MICHAEL S. WILDER AND
TIMOTHY PAUL JONES

A couple of years ago, an individual who thought he might be called to pastoral ministry informed me (Jones), "I love to teach, and I want to preach — but I can't stand people." He went on to describe his dream position: to provide a polished exposition of Scripture every Sunday morning, to decide the church's vision and direction, but never to deal directly with the people in the congregation. It was a pleasant-sounding dream with one fatal flaw: no such position exists in the very Scriptures that he claimed he wanted to proclaim.

What this young man needed wasn't merely an improvement in his people skills — though, frankly, he could have used that too. What he needed was to understand the difference between cattle and sheep.

Throughout Scripture, sheep provide a primary metaphor for God's people (1 Kgs 22:17; Ps 77:20) and God himself is the great shepherd (Gen 49:24; Ps 23:1). Yet the imagery doesn't end there. Divinely designated leaders are seen as shepherds too (Num 27:15-18; 2 Sam 5:2). In the New Testament, "shepherds," or "pastors," becomes a term to describe the church's God-ordained overseers (Eph 4:11).

So what does all this have to do with differentiating cattle and sheep? Cattle might meander among the oaks of Bashan or find themselves being fattened in pens (Amos 4:1; 6:4); either way, their tending did not require their keepers to live among them. Sheep, on the other hand, need a shepherd, and shepherds live among their sheep. When the shepherd fails to guide his sheep, the flock becomes fragmented and vulnerable (1 Kgs 22:17; 2 Chr 18:16; Zech 10:2).

The young man who declared he wanted to be a pastor but didn't want to deal with people was contradicting himself. You can't be a shepherd without living among the sheep.

The struggle to live as a shepherd is not new, of course. Leaders who failed to care for their flocks were, in fact, part of the problem that the prophet Ezekiel saw in the sixth century B.C. when he looked at the rulers of Israel. Ezekiel's inspired pronouncement did not point his people toward some new leadership technique; instead, the prophet pointed them toward the sacrificial life of a leader yet to come.

SHEPHERDS OR SOVEREIGNS?

Even in the nations that surrounded Israel, "shepherd" functioned as a metaphor for rulers and gods – but Israel's kings were called to shepherd God's people in a very different way. The kings of Israel were never to present themselves as royal owners of the flock. God alone was the Lord of Israel, and the people were his property. The kings were under-shepherds. Like shepherds in the field tending the flock of a higher lord, the kings were responsible to live among their subjects, to guide them and to guard them for God's glory.

But the kings of Israel and Judah failed. In the decades after David, they began to treat God's people as their own property. According to Ezekiel, they failed to feed God's flock (Ezek 34:2). Instead of serving among the people of God's flock, these kings "ruled them" with "force and harshness" like Pharaoh in the days of Moses (Ezek 34:4; Exod 1:13-14). The protectors became predators. The people became like sheep without a shepherd, scattered and slaughtered for the sake of their rulers (Ezek 34:3, 6).

Fixing this failure would require something far more radical than a tweak in the shepherding habits of human kings. The sole solution would be the arrival of God himself. The Lord of the flock would live among his people as their shepherd (Ezek 34:12). God himself would show up to seek out his scattered sheep, to separate the sleek from the weak and to fill the feed-troughs of the oppressors with judgment (Ezek 34:11, 16-22). Once again, it would be clear that these people were the property of God alone.

God did not, however, give up on working through the offspring of Eve. He predicted through Ezekiel that he would raise up a human ruler as well: one like David, who would live not as a sovereign but as a servant, a prince, and an under-shepherd (Ezek 34:23-24). This ruler would also live "among" his flock, and God himself would remain "with them" forever (Ezek 34:24, 28-30).

All of this was partly fulfilled in the post-exile period — but only partly. On this side of the cross and empty tomb, it's clear that Jesus provided the ultimate fulfillment of both predictions. As God enfleshed, he was the rightful Lord and King of his people. Yet he willingly became not only the servant and the shepherd but also the sacrificial lamb. The shepherd was stricken by God for sins that were not his own and then rose to life to gather his own from every nation (Zech 13:9; Matt 26:31-32; 28:19; John 10:14-18; Rev 7:9-17).

As he gathers his own, Jesus the exalted shepherd king has chosen once again to work through human shepherds. In the Gospels, the apostles began as sheep (Matt 10:16) but wound up as shepherds (John 21:15-18) who then recognized other God-appointed men as shepherds of this flock (Eph 4:11; 1 Pet 5:1-2). Yet now, as in the days of Ezekiel, God himself remains the chief shepherd, the true owner of the sheep (Heb 13:20; 1 Pet 2:25, 5:4). Pastors are not lords of the sheep but servants of the King, called to imitate the chief shepherd.

IMITATING THE CHIEF SHEPHERD

So what does all of this mean for pastoral leaders in the church of Jesus Christ?

1. *Shepherd leadership calls for feeding the flock.* The primary responsibility of the shepherd is to provide nourishment for the flock (Ezek 34:2). So it is in church life, the pastor must consider that his leadership is most strikingly demonstrated through his teaching and preaching ministry. The chief shepherd was known as one who taught with great authority (John 1:29; Matt 7:28-29). Remember when Jesus invited his disciples to retreat to a deserted place? When they arrived, the spot was no longer deserted because the people had anticipated where Jesus might be headed. Compassion welled up within Jesus when he saw the people because "they were like sheep without a shepherd." His immediate response is telling: "he began to teach them many things" (Mark 6:34).

Later, along the shores of Galilee, Jesus prepared breakfast for the disciples. This post-resurrection appearance concluded with Jesus asking Simon Peter three times, "Do you love me?" The response to Peter's affirmations of love were "Feed *my* lambs. ... Tend *my* sheep. ... Feed *my* sheep." Peter was reminded that he had been called to serve Christ by being a servant who feeds the flock. It was through feeding God's people he was to demonstrate authentic love for the chief shepherd.

Pastoral leadership is rooted in the responsibility of living as an under-shepherd with eyes fixed on the chief shepherd. True compassion for people and love for God compels the pastoral leader to make Christ known through the teaching of God's Word.

2. *Shepherd leadership calls for guarding the flock.* In God's rebuke against Israel's leaders, he indicted them as predators rather than protectors. The rulers of Israel were devouring the flock for their own gain so that God's sheep were scattered and became "food for all the wild beasts" (Ezek 34:3, 5, 8). God, who would reverse the evils of the leaders, declared that he would rescue his sheep and give them rest so that they would no longer be prey (Ezek 34:12, 14, 15, 22). A mark of divine leadership is protection. So it is with shepherd leaders in Christ's church.

3. *Shepherd leadership leads to sacrificial service among the people.* Jesus, the model shepherd, makes this clear in his words to the Pharisees: "the good shepherd lays down his life for the sheep" (John 10:11). This is exactly what Christ did on our behalf through his finished work on the cross. It is no wonder then that, immediately after calling Peter to feed his sheep, the resurrected Jesus also called Peter to follow him to the point of death (John 21:18-19).

The difficulty is that there are pastors who choose to live as self-centered shepherds, much like the rulers described in Ezekiel. But there is another category of shepherds in the church — those who are *flock-centered*. This descriptor sounds positive, but it too falls short of authentic imitation of the chief shepherd. These leaders encourage their sheep and may even know their sheep, but they are marked by a desire to keep the flock happy and satisfied. They keep peace in the fold at any price. This well intended desire can lead to unwillingness to deal with sin or false teachings. The result is contentment to gather with the 99 – and to gather more "99s"— without seeking or correcting the one who wanders (Ezek 34:4-5, 8; Matt 18:12-14). This approach to shepherding ultimately produces weakened churches and a diminished display of God's holiness and glory.

Leaders who understand their role as shepherds do not peer

down at their people from a holy hayloft and drop an occasional bale of sustenance in the form of a finely crafted homily. Neither do they allow their flocks to live in false peace. Shepherd leaders live among their people and pay "careful attention ... to all the flock" (Acts 20:28). They see themselves neither as sovereigns over their churches nor as hirelings of their churches but as under-shepherds of the living God.

This article is adapted and abridged from the forthcoming The God Who Goes Before You: A Biblical Theology of Leadership, *by Michael S. Wilder and Timothy Paul Jones (Nashville: B&H Academic, 2018).*

04

Leaders, find your identity in Christ: Be careful not to find your identity in what you do

As you grow in your skills and leadership, be careful to not find your identity in what you're particularly good at doing.

BY JEREMY RHODEN

As you grow in your skills and leadership, be careful to not find your identity in what you're particularly good at doing. If you begin to lead, and if you show a type of grit that is befitting of a person of God, and you're making those decisions, and if you begin to be recognized for being gifted in that arena, you are in the dangerous spot of easily letting that gift define who you are as a man or woman. It's where your confidence comes from. It's where you're most comfortable with who you are. It's where you know what to do. It's where you have direction. Perhaps this reveals itself most on your days off of work. You know the feeling I'm talking about. It's when you wake up on your day off and you feel kind of lost and you don't know precisely what to do and you kind of look forward to getting back to work or back to the role where you know you are gifted. Be careful! This might be a sign of finding your identity in the wrong place. How do you guard against finding identity in your leadership and work? Contemplate your true identity.

- You are justified by his grace as a gift, through the redemption that is in Christ Jesus.
- You are dead to sin and alive to God in Christ Jesus.
- You are the recipient of the free gift of God which is eternal life in Christ Jesus.
- You are the ones that now know no condemnation for you are in Christ Jesus.
- You are the ones that the Spirit of life has set free from the law of sin and death in Christ Jesus.
- You are the ones that neither height nor depth, nor anything else in all creation, will be able to separate from the love of God in Christ Jesus.

Your identity is to be found in Christ Jesus alone. Do you want to lead well? Then you must not be tempted by what worldly leadership has to offer in this life.

THE BENEFIT OF IDENTITY IN CHRIST

Guarding yourself against improper identity in those leadership roles allows you to transition out of roles when the time comes. There will come a point in certain leadership roles where the most God-glorifying thing and the thing that best serves those around you is for you to transition out of that role. If your identity is wrapped up in Christ, this will come much easier. If your identity is wrapped up in what you've become good at doing, this will be a painful process for you and those around you.

DO STUFF WITH YOUR HANDS

As you grow in leadership, much of your work becomes knowledge work. In our western civilization, much of our work is research, or computer work, or teaching, or things that are not done with the hands. Make sure that you encourage yourself with occasional concrete and definitive work. This is more than completing a checklist. This is starting a physical task and completing it.

Maybe it's building a treehouse for your kids. Maybe it's running or gardening. Think here of Ronald Reagan at his ranch taking care of the land. It's something concrete that can be measured. You can physically see improvement. You can work on specific aspects to affect improvement. Encourage yourself. Take a break from the knowledge work that is before you. These physical tasks have a way of simultaneously humbling you and encouraging you all at once.

ASK THE LORD FOR WISDOM

Remember to ask the Lord for wisdom and guidance. When I was young, a mentor and I were speaking and parted ways on a Sunday morning. And I was talking with my friends in youth group, he ran up to me and said, "Jeremiah, I forgot to tell you, every time you sit down to read the Word, or even when you're reading something like theology, ask for the Spirit to guide your heart and mind and illuminate God's truths to you." That has always stuck with me. And I pray every time I sit down to read the word that the Lord would send His spirit to guide my heart and mind. The same goes for tasks that you set out to do. Ask the Lord for wisdom and guidance in your leadership every day. Every day at work, I ask for the Lord's wisdom in guiding our company. Remember, these do not have to be complex and amazing prayers with wonderful insights. You're just a person.

And you're talking to the almighty creator of the universe. It's a simple request. Ask for wisdom. He knows your needs. Go about your day. But be consistent about praying for wisdom. James 1:5 says if any of you lacks wisdom, let him ask God, who gives generously to all without reproach, and it will be given him.

WORK HARD, THEN WORK SMART

You've heard it said, "work smart, not hard." I would say, work smart, yes. But first, work hard. In our rush to become leaders, we're often prone to skipping the step of working hard. There is no better way to understand how to work smarter until you have done the very hard work of what it takes to get the job done. There is no better way to learn how to lead those under your leadership until you know precisely what it takes to get the job done. This will increase your understanding of what it means to be efficient in that particular role. So, if you're a dad, help your kids clean their room from time to time. If you're a manager, help unload the truck from time to time. Also, engaging in this hard work leads to the grit and perseverance that is needed later on in successful leadership.

ENJOY THE LEADERS AROUND YOU

Guard yourself from secretly delighting in the demise of your co-leaders or being jealous of their victory. When you decide to lead, you will find yourself in the company of talented individuals. Get used to it and enjoy their success. Do not be jealous and insecure because of this. If you're following your biblical decision filtration system, that we spoke of earlier, you'll be able to weed this out through careful meditation on God's word.

Are you glorifying God by comparing yourself in this way? Are you serving them by thinking this way? A helpful note here is to meditate on Moses and Joshua's relationship in Numbers 11, where Joshua is jealous for Moses to be the only one who prophesies and Moses says, "are you jealous for my sake? I wish that all the Lord's people were prophets and that the Lord would put his Spirit on them." There is no room for jealousy in godly leadership!

GUARD YOUR FRIENDSHIPS

As you progress in leadership, you are also progressing in age. As you age and become better at what you do, this creates a recipe

20

for loneliness. You find yourself in a spot where, because of your giftings or because of your busyness, or whatever it might be, you wake up one day to realize that you don't have a friend that you can confide in. You can find yourself in a lonely spot quickly. Be careful to identify your role as a friend to those around you and work on being a good friend. Seeking out close friendships is part of healthy leadership.

HAVE A SHORT MEMORY

Finally, as a leader, you need to be quick to accept the blame for what has gone wrong. However, do not dwell on failures in an unhealthy way. Learn from them and wipe the slate clean. There is no better example of this than king David. Read and re-read the books of Samuel. Learn from but do not be distracted by your failures. More importantly than that, do not be distracted by your victories and successes. Nothing detracts from progress in leadership more than reveling over one's own brief success. A good leader has a short memory when it comes to failures but he has an even shorter memory when it comes to his victories. Properly focusing on Christ and God's glory have the humbling effect of shaking failures and victories away so that we don't depend on them in improper ways.

05

Two Scripture passages every church leader needs every day

Meditate on these texts to nourish your faithfulness and silence your anxiety.

BY JEFF ROBINSON

L ocal church ministry, whether you are serving as a pastor in an established church, as a church planter, a missionary, an elder, in a staff position, or other, is a little like baseball — it's an exercise in managing failure. Here's what I mean: Ted Williams, arguably the greatest hitter in professional baseball history, finished with a .344 career batting average. Williams, nicknamed the "Splendid Splinter," succeeded only 34 times out of every 100 times he came to bat — he made an out in those other 66 trips to home plate.

That's a lot of failure. Ministry can be like that — or at least it can feel like it.

You preach God's Word week in and week out, and more often than not, you don't see the change that takes place in people's hearts. Sanctification is gradual, comes over time, and is usually invisible as it happens. Thus, preaching is not like mowing the lawn or building a table — there is no visible "product" at the end of the sermon. God has called us to faithfully proclaim his Word and leave the results to him — the "leaving the results" part is not easy for people with iPhones and microwave ovens. Anxiety can crash upon the shores of a minister's life with the impact of a deadly tsunami.

Preaching weekly can leave us feeling a little like the mythical Greek king Sisyphus who tricked Persephone, goddess of the underworld. For his shenanigans, Sisyphus was sentenced to an eternity of repeatedly pushing a boulder up a steep hill, only to watch it roll back to the bottom.

You prepare the sermon, preach the sermon, prepare the sermon, preach the sermon, wash, rinse, repeat. Every Monday, discouragement lurks like the unholiest of ghosts just outside the study door.

To build a dam that will restrain the storm of anxiety and chase away the apparition of discouragement, you need a strong dose of God's truth daily applied. I want to suggest two texts that have helped me, texts I preach to myself regularly as a guard against two major thieves that threaten to rob me of joy as both a believer and a pastor.

MATTHEW 6:25-34: A STRONG ANTIDOTE FOR YOUR ANXIETY

Jesus's thesis is as easy to discern as it is consoling to comprehend: Because God is your God, you don't have to be anxious about your life. Our Lord here presents an argument from lesser to greater: Since God feeds the birds of the air, he clothes the flowers of the field, how much more can he be trusted to take care of his people?

Yet we worry. And when we worry, we have experienced failure at two levels: a failure to understand that God is our Father and a failure to exhibit childlike faith — what Jesus here calls "little faith." Jesus shows the absurdity of worry for God's people, a reality that ought to be doubly true for those who get their living through studying and teaching his Word: Worry cannot add even 3,600 seconds to your life. The person who dies at age 75 has lived more than 650,000 hours, so adding one to the span would seem an easy proposition, yet the Lord says we can't do it. Worry adds nothing to us. I take great comfort in what Jesus concludes in his admonition in 6:34:

> Therefore, do not be anxious about tomorrow, for tomorrow will be anxious for itself. Sufficient for the day is its own trouble.

As ministers, we must trust and obey what Jesus says in verse 33 after he has told his audience not to worry about what they will eat or drink or wear:

> But seek first the kingdom of God and his righteousness, and all these things will be added to you.

Ministers — and people in the pew — are to make God's redemptive rule and right relationship with him the highest priorities of their lives, and we must concern ourselves with today, not tomorrow, trusting that God will provide for us, our families, and our congregation. Jesus's words here need not be limited in their application to the provision of physical needs — though that's clearly in view and is of profound comfort to us — but may be applied to our need for spiritual sustenance as well.

MARK 4:26-29: NOURISHING FOOD FOR YOUR FAITHFULNESS

Our Lord's words here ought to liberate us from the success syndrome — measuring ministry success on purely human scales. I pray through this pithy parable virtually every Saturday night before I head to the pulpit on Sunday. It is a reminder of who builds God's kingdom.

> And [Jesus] said, "The kingdom of God is as if a man should scatter seed on the ground. He sleeps and rises night and day, and the

25

> seed sprouts and grows; he knows not how. The earth produces
> by itself, first the blade, then the ear, then the full grain in the ear."

For the man of God, here is the liberating truth in this passage: Everything is God's doing. Are the people in your church growing spiritually? God is doing it. Are there lost people coming to Christ? God is doing it. Are there new members joining the church? God is doing it. Are you in a drier season in which nothing seems to be happening? God is doing it. Keep planting the seed.

What does the sower do after he sows the seed? *He goes to bed.* The sower is responsible to sow, not to make the seed grow. While he sleeps, the kingdom of God grows. The sower doesn't assist it. He doesn't even understand it: "the seed sprouts and grows, *he knows not how.*"

I relish this parable's teaching because it reminds me that I am only responsible to sow the seed faithfully. By no means is this a call to passivity. Do we diligently seek the conversion of lost people? Certainly. Do we labor intensely to see lives changed? Of course. That's why you surrendered to ministry in the first place. But is God's undershepherd under pressure to make it happen? By no means. If hearts are to change, God must do it, and elsewhere Jesus promises to build his church and even the power of hell will not prevail over it (Matt 16:18). God is sovereign over my congregation, and I must rest in that.

That precious promise drives away anxiety and discouragement on those days when nothing seems to be happening in ministry, when I'm sowing but nothing seems to be growing. If I have been faithful, I can plant the seed and rest easy in Christ, knowing his Spirit will cause the seed to germinate and take root in human hearts, in soil made good by the Holy Spirit (Mark 4:1-9). I need not pressure the people, harangue them, cajole them, or wring my hands in perplexity. This parable comforts me with the truth Luther understood, the truth that was the catalyst for one of the greatest revivals in church history 500 years ago: "The Word did everything, I did nothing." Indeed.

GIVE THANKS

Brothers, this Thanksgiving week, let us give thanks to our faithful, mighty Lord that he has given us these precious texts to help us beat back the twin monsters of anxiety and discouragement. May the God of peace give you grace to sow the seed, trust him wholly, and rest in the promises of his all-powerful Word.

27

06

Every leader needs this kind of friend

Three marks of true Christian friendship

BY MATTHEW J. HALL

D oes leadership have to be a lonely venture? Listen to some of the most prominent voices on leadership, within Christian circles and beyond, and you will be reminded that leadership more often than not brings with it a measure of aloneness.

The leader will, at times, find himself or herself standing alone. And the experience can make one feel as though there is no one else who fully understands the burden of decisions and pressure. A 2012 survey reported half of all CEOs expressed feelings of loneliness in their work. Christian leaders are not immune.

Though there are unique burdens to bear, friendship is essential for a Christian leader. I remain a relatively young man with a limited leadership role entrusted to me. But in my experience and reflection, I am convinced friendship is vital to joyful and effective leadership. Friendship is more than a luxury afforded only to the fortunate few. It is part of what it means to be human, to live a good life. And leaders are not, thanks be to God, exempt from that divine design.

Friendship is more than a luxury afforded only to the fortunate few. It is part of what it means to be human.

As historian Martin Marty wisely noted, "The quality of friendships or the absence of them tells more about the lives of great people than most other features." In the hyper-individualistic

West, I fear we miss this ancient truth. But consider it for a moment. Many great figures in Christian history depended on friendship in their vocation.

Here are three lessons I continue to learn by God's grace, and will for the rest of my life.

1. A TRUE FRIEND TELLS YOU THE TRUTH

Our relationships mirror the divine fellowship. And that kind of friendship is built on truth telling. The Christian faith holds this as integral. Fellowship with God requires truth telling, finding that the God of the cosmos has spoken his Word to us, revealing himself to his creatures as an act of friendship. He is therefore fully trustworthy, worthy of adoration and faith.

At their truest and best, our human friendships reflect this reality. Friends tell us the truth about others, ourselves, and the gospel.

Leadership is predicated on forming judgments and determining a wise course of action. These necessarily involve judgments about others, including those we're called to lead. I've often found my judgments misinformed or incomplete, and I needed a true friend to provide me with a more accurate perspective. When someone disappoints the leader, it's easy to dismiss them or assume the worst.

But a friend explains there is more going on than meets the eye. Friends help us assume the best about others. And when needed, they also caution and warn against those who present themselves as allies, but have set themselves against the organization's mission. We need both. Only a friend will do that for a leader.

Friends are also necessary to tell us the truth about ourselves. Like all humans, leaders are tempted to believe their own press. Sin and pride make us quick to underestimate our weakness and overestimate our abilities and virtues. A colleague may reinforce those blind spots, whether out of unvarnished sycophancy or fear of disappointment. But a friend steps in and, with near prophetic courage, calls us to account. Do you see your friends as gifts of grace to protect you from yourself?

Most importantly, a Christian friend tells us the truth about the gospel. They keep the good news before us in concrete and personal terms. A friend reminds the leader that they're a sinner, that they need daily grace, and that any good thing — even their leadership ability — is entirely a gift. A friend reminds us that the most important thing about us is not our organizational success or status, but our identity in Christ. A friend presses us to hope in what is enduring, not in what is fleeting.

2. A TRUE FRIEND IS MOTIVATED BY LOVE, NOT SELF-INTEREST

Friendship is preferential love. Not only do we prefer some above others, but Christian friendship means we prefer others — our friends — above ourselves.

We can be friendly with many people, but true friendship is rare. Our lives are embedded within institutions and organizations that, by necessity, demand a culture of friendliness. We see colleagues in the hallway, at meetings, at social functions. And certainly a broad culture of warmth, courtesy, and amicable goodwill is an essential characteristic of healthy organizational ethos. But true friendship that extends beyond professional conversations and sheer transactionalism is a rare gift.

The reason for this is an ancient truth rooted in the beginning of all things. We are made for God, to be sure, but we are also made for others. At the center of this design is the dynamic force of love. Self-interest draws us to see others as opportunities for transactions, beings from whom I can make a withdrawal to satisfy my needs for security, affirmation, validation, and pleasure. But love, which is part of the overflow of Trinitarian relations, is not self-seeking. It is self-giving.

The commodification of friendship is seen in the countless ways we look to people to render us some sort of service. Instead of mirroring the intra-Trinitarian fellowship of joy, friendship is traded for something far less. Because of sin, all of us are prone to distorted and skewed realities in our friendships. But Christian leaders need to be mindful of the specific ways self-interest can subtly masquerade as friendship. It may yield something that has the appearance of friendship, but is a lethal counterfeit.

3. A TRUE FRIEND REMAINS WHEN YOUR LEADERSHIP FAILS

At some point, your leadership will wane. Age will bring this about naturally, but failure has a way of accelerating the process too. It's one thing to find yourself in a season of success surrounded by many who appear to be friends. But what happens when your company fails, your organization goes bankrupt, or your reputation is no longer about competence and skill?

The Bible presents a picture of friendship enduring: "A friend loves at all times, and a brother is born for adversity" (Prov 17:17).

While your siblings are there in moments of crisis, your friends are present in all life's ups and downs. We don't get to choose our siblings; they are providentially assigned. But there is a voluntary nature to friendship that makes it all the sweeter. A friend can reject and spurn us. That elective dynamic makes friendship a risky venture, but one that holds potential for unspeakable joy and love.

If you're a leader and think you're surrounded by friends, don't be too sure. On the other hand, don't let awareness of the fickle and opportunistic nature of professional relationships make you crudely cynical. A far more biblical and wise tact is to approach relationships with a measure of realism. Cynicism will compound your loneliness and make you distrust others, robbing you of opportunities for the joy of friendship. Realism will give you a clear-eyed appreciation for genuine friendship and protect you from disillusionment when others disappoint you.

Friendship is a risky venture, but it holds potential for unspeakable joy and love.

A true friend will be there when all else is gone. This kind of loyalty and steadfastness is a sign, pointing us to an even greater reality — to the one who perfectly embodies friendship. It surely is as the hymn writer said, "Jesus! What a friend for sinners! Jesus! Lover of my soul / Friends may fail me, foes assail me, he, my Savior, makes me whole."

ACQUAINTANCES VS. TRUE FRIENDS

You likely have fewer friends than you realize. In an age of social media and pseudo-friendships, there is a noxious counterfeit that easily misleads us. You may have hundreds of acquaintances, but chances are you have only three or four true friends. If that sounds disappointing, perhaps you've misunderstood the nature of friendship and so are routinely frustrated by misplaced expectations.

Many of us have confused what C. S. Lewis clarified in distinguishing between friendship and companionship: Friendship arises out of mere companionship when two or more of the companions discover that they have in common some insight or interest or even taste which the others do not share and which, till that moment, each believed to be his own unique treasure (or burden). The typical expression of opening Friendship would be something like, "What? You too? I thought I was the only one."

This article was originally published at The Gospel Coalition.

07

Making the most of Sunday morning conversations

It is a constant juggling match that most pastors feel they fail at most of the time.

BY BRIAN CROFT

I t is one of the great dilemmas every Sunday for the pastor. To whom do I speak with and for how long? Many pastors stand at a doorway after the morning service to greet those who are leaving. Others stay down front inviting folks to come and speak with the pastor to ask questions about the sermon.

It is a constant juggling match that most pastors feel they fail at most of the time.

What adds to the madness is the person who aggressively hunts the pastor down after the service and feels entitled to his undivided attention for a long time. This is the person that feels a complete disregard for others that are usually patiently waiting in line. In our church, this person usually is someone who has come in off the street, does not know any better, and wants clothes, food, or money.

This could also be a church member in your church who does not choose the best time to hash out their marital problems with the pastor. Yet, we still do not want to miss any opportunities for ministry to these needy folks, especially if they are souls under our care. What do you do? Here are three suggestions:

1. GIVE THEM A MOMENT

We can take this caution too far and not bother with these kinds of people at all. That is wrong. Regardless who they are, where they come from, or what their reason is to talk to "the pastor," give them a moment so you can find out the basics about them and their need. It will help you know how to proceed with them and possibly involve another leader.

2. TRAIN OTHER LEADERS TO STEP IN TO HELP

After preaching and concluding a very important ordination service in our church, I was approached by a homeless woman who walked up to the platform to speak with me before anybody else could reach me. She began to tell me about her problems, and they were many. She needed serious help, and had I stood there for two hours, she would have continued to talk that long.

One of our leaders noticed what was happening and realized that was not the best way for me to spend my time as many were waiting to talk to me.

He realized someone else could help. So, this leader came and took the initiative to politely take her to someone else to help her. Train your leaders to notice these moments as folks come asking for food or clothes so they can come to intervene. For me to pass them on to a deacon who is better equipped to help them in that moment is a tremendous blessing to all involved.

If a person is upset with the decision you made at the member's meeting earlier in the week and is making a scene while berating you about it, find another pastor to come and help take that difficult situation for you. Then, you are able to move to the next person. Train your pastors, deacons, and other leaders to think this way and be aware of what is happening, and with discernment, jump in if needed.

3. REMEMBER THE SHEEP MOST COMMONLY NEGLECTED

It is hard to pick and choose in these moments. That is why most pastors feel like they fail at it. However, what we can be sure of, is the sheep most neglected are those who do not fight for your time and do not wait in large lines to talk with you.

They do not want to add to burden for you.

Be willing to ask someone to set an appointment with you at the office that week to talk about the issue that will require a longer conversation than you can have on Sunday morning. This gives the pastor the ability to prioritize seeking out that passive sheep that needs your care.

Pastors should be deliberate enough and leading conversations enough that we do not allow our time to be dominated on Sundays by someone else. Be gracious. Be wise. But choose who you will talk to and for how long. If you do not choose, trust me, someone else will choose for you.

37

08

How to deal with a church disrupter

Five strategies for dealing with members who disrupt church unity

BY THOM S. RAINER

He is in almost every church.

In fact, the "he" may be a "she," but I'll use the masculine pronoun for simplicity.

He is the church disrupter. Unlike church bullies, the disrupter rarely attacks leaders directly. He is good about stirring up dissension, but he seems to always feel like "God led me to do it." He can have a gregarious and pleasant personality (unlike the typical church bully), and can thus attract a following for a season.

The disrupter is just that. He disrupts the unity of the church. He disrupts the outward focus of the church. And he disrupts the plans of church leadership. So what are some key traits to watch in church disrupters?

Here are six:

1. He often seeks positions in the church so he can get attention. So be wary if he asks to lead the student group or the praise team or become chairman of the finance committee. He loves to exert his negative influence through key and visible positions.

2. He often votes "no" in business meetings. Again, this tactic is yet another attempt to get attention.

3. He loves to say, "People are saying . . ." He wants you to think his issue is more widespread than it really is. Another approach is, "If we had a secret ballot vote, there would be a lot more dissenters."

4. He tries to get followers at the church for his cause of the moment. That is another reason he seeks positions of influence in the church.

5. He often assures the pastor and other church leaders how much he loves them and supports them. And then he goes and stabs them in the back.

6. He loves to use "facts" loosely for his case or cause. Accuracy is neither required nor expected.

So how should pastors and other church leaders address the problem of church disrupters? Allow me to suggest a few ideas.

- Determine you will love them as Christ loves you and them. It's tough, but it can be done in Christ's strength.
- Pray for them. Seriously.
- Be on the watch for them. They can be manipulative and deceptive; they can cause chaos before you see it coming.
- Get other leaders to help you address the disrupters and their disruption. But, be aware, they will be shocked you perceive them that way.
- As soon as possible, get them out of key leadership positions. They are a problem now, but they can become toxic later.

I have my theories on why church disrupters act the way they do, but that is a topic for another post. In the meantime, be wary of church disrupters. But love them and pray for them anyway.

That is the way Christ would respond.

09

Four men you should take to the mission field and three you should leave behind

Every missionary going to the field must make sure to take four men with him, and leave three others behind.

BY M. DAVID SILLS

Every missionary going to the field must make sure to take four men with him, and leave three others behind. Individualistic Western missionary candidates are often so self-sufficient and satisfy so much of their need for social interaction online that the idea of taking others with them is a new thought and seems intrusive. But each of these men are essential members of every effective mission team.

When Frank and Marie Drown, missionaries to Ecuador's Shuar indigenous peoples, left for the field in the 1940s, president Gordon Weiss of the Gospel Missionary Union gave wise counsel to the departing missionaries. His advice was not just wise for the 1940s; it is just as pertinent today. He told them that four men must go with them to the mission field: the spiritual man, the intellectual man, the social man, and the physical man.

TAKE FOUR

Let's consider these four men.

1. The physical man: Missionaries need to develop and maintain robust physical health to survive and thrive in the rigors of the mission field. Changes in altitude, climate, food, water, demanding schedules, exposure to tropical diseases, amoebas, and parasites can sideline or send home a missionary in short order.

2. The intellectual man: Missionaries who cultivate a keen and consecrated practical intelligence learn the culture and language more easily and with much less stress. Sharpening your intellect to be interested in your surroundings, how things work, and why they are as they are will help you in life when your former social cues, normal routines, and second-nature tasks no longer work.

3. The social man: Missionaries need to love people, enjoy being with them, and look for opportunities to make personal relationships. The ability to make deep friendships out of casual social contacts is profoundly helpful for personal evangelism, discipleship, church planting, and mentoring others.

4. The spiritual man: Developing a strong spiritual life maintained by regular and consistent prayer and Bible study habits is the most important of these four. Remember that your battle is not against flesh and blood but rather against spiritual powers that are to be engaged with spiritual weapons. Success in your Christian life and missionary career has a lot to do with getting as close to Jesus as you can, and staying there.

LEAVE THREE BEHIND

To Mr. Weiss's four men who must go with the missionary, I would caution that there are three men who must be left behind: a ladies' man, a man's man, and a selfish man:

1. **The ladies' man.** A ladies' man is one who dresses and acts in such a way as to attract the ladies' attention and seeks to be charming in his interaction with them. They are his focus.

2. **The man's man.** A man's man is one who is so focused on sports, hunting, fishing, and other manly activities that he cannot relate to others such as widows, children, or young families. He is either out with the boys on his latest competitive activity or he is still talking about the last one. He lives to make other men think he is the pinnacle of machismo and manliness.

3. **The selfish man.** A selfish man is one who lives for his own desires. He is often lazy, gluttonous, wasteful, and spends excessively on himself. He is insensitive to others, eats in front of the hungry, refuses to serve others if it cuts into his plans, or flaunts his money and possessions in front of poorer people. Certainly most missionaries aren't such an "ugly American." But some live lavish lifestyles compared to their national friends, drive the nicest cars, put their kids in the most expensive international schools, and openly talk about it all. They justify this lifestyle as what they deserve for so much sacrifice, and never consider how it hinders their impact. A selfish man lives for himself.

FOUR MINUS THREE

Effective missionaries have always found that taking the first four men with them and leaving the next three behind results in the best missionary. Four minus three equals the best one. The spiritual man, the intellectual man, the social man, and the physical man minus the ladies' man, the man's man, and the selfish man equals God's man.

The best missionary will be the one who lives for God with both eyes set on pleasing him, maintaining a heart for God and a mind for truth. When we imagine God deciding to use a man, looking down on earth to choose a missionary, or desiring a man to serve him and others, we should envision this kind of man. Missionaries are men and women of great gifts and abilities, but their strength and effectiveness are dependent on the God who has called and sent them. Be God's man.

Both men and women have been, are now, and will always be godly and effective missionaries until Christ returns. This short article is a talk prepared as a charge to a group of deploying male missionaries, thus the references to men and the use of masculine pronouns. Please know that I do not mean to be sexist or to imply that only men should be missionaries. Feel free to exchange specific masculine references for other pronouns, or the word "person," as you read. These principles are applicable to all missionaries.

10

Essential attributes of an effective worship leader

Leading a task that engages a holy God with such eternal implications should not be handled lightly.

BY SCOTT CONNELL

I have the privilege of training worship leaders. This means I have the task of preparing musicians to lead their congregations in something that they will continue to do in eternity. Done well, this act should help teach people how to live in faith and to one day die with hope.

Leading a task that engages a holy God with such eternal implications should not be handled lightly. It takes a substantive person to plan, prepare, and lead what should be a substantive act.

Here are seven things I believe a worship leader must demonstrate in order to be effective for this significant task:

1. MUSICAL TALENT

This is the only characteristic on the list that must be present at birth. Some people have a gift for music and others do not. For those that do, that talent must be developed and refined. This takes time and work, but the combination of these two demonstrates the presence of talent. Effective worship leaders practice and get better.

"Sing to him a new song; play skillfully" (Ps 33:3).

2. TEACHABILITY

Regardless of how talented a worship leader is, teachability is always required. Good worship leaders are continually learning and seeking instruction. A worship leader who resists instruction will be a poor teacher himself. Effective worship leaders strive to be teachable.

"Poverty and disgrace come to him who ignores instruction, but whoever heeds reproof is honored" (Prov 13:18).

3. BIBLICAL KNOWLEDGE

This is a characteristic that everyone begins life with a total absence of. It is necessary to create a lifelong appetite for God's Word. Every week worship leaders point people to God while also representing the character and works of God in song and speech. Too many do so out of theological and biblical ignorance.

Effective worship leaders develop a reservoir of biblical truth within them so they can speak and lead intelligently.

"All Scripture is breathed out by God and profitable for teaching, for reproof, for correction, and for training in righteousness, that the man of God may be competent, equipped for every good work" (2 Tim 3:16).

4. CHARACTER

The hypocrisy of a duplicitous life on any platform will eventually be revealed. Standing on a platform to lead worship is essentially saying "Follow me while I follow Christ." Perfection is unattainable for anyone, but sanctification is honest about sin and progressive in growth because it comes from following Christ intentionally. Unfortunately, talent has a way of taking musicians farther than their character can sustain them. Effective worship leaders grow in godliness.

"For the Lord sees not as man sees: man looks on the outward appearance, but the Lord looks on the heart" (1 Sam 16:17b).

5. PASSION

Worship should have an appropriate and authentic emotional component. I am not referring to pep rally emotionalism, but neither should there be the appearance of apathy or disinterest. Worship should reflect deep-seated joy, true brokenness over sin, and authentic (even euphoric) gratefulness for the savior. Effective worship leaders cultivate the capacity to be appropriately affected emotionally because worship is an unparalleled journey of enjoying ultimate fulfillment at Christ's expense.

"*My heart and flesh sing for joy to the living God*" (Ps 84:2b).

6. HUMILITY

This may be the most elusive characteristic on the list. Performing music can tend to make musicians arrogant. A musical skill can become a motive for boasting in an otherwise reserved individual. The types of thoughts that can come to mind while leading worship can be startling if evaluated honestly. Effective worship leaders pursue God's glory over their own glory.

"*God opposes the proud but gives grace to the humble*" (James 4:6).

7. LOVE FOR THE CHURCH

This can often be the most forgotten item on the list. If allowed, love for music can eclipse love for the people. The true allegiance of our affections will be on display in numerous decisions that we make every week. Effective worship leaders examine their motives and advance strategies that make music a servant, not a master.

"*Love one another with brotherly affection. Outdo one another in showing honor*" (Rom 12:10).

Being a worship leader is a journey. Proper orientation in these things reflects one's capability and fitness for being used in a role that none of us truly deserves to hold. We serve at God's pleasure. Enter humbly, grow intentionally.

47

11

Follow Spurgeon's example in reading good books

One of the reasons Spurgeon was so rich in language and full in doctrinal substance is that he was always immersed in a great book.

BY RAY RHODES JR.

What did Spurgeon read? He read all sorts of books. He read the Bible, the newspaper, Christian classics, history, biography, and fiction. He averaged reading six substantive books each week. Most of those books were weighty Puritan works.

John Piper writes:

> I think one of the reasons Spurgeon was so rich in language and full in doctrinal substance and strong in the spirit, in spite of his despondency and his physical oppression and his embattlements, is that he was always immersed in a great book—six a week. We cannot match that number. But we can always be walking with some great "see-er" of God. I walked with Owen most of the year on and off little by little and felt myself strengthened by a great grasp of God's reality.

A primary reason that Spurgeon was such a great writer was due to his reading habits. W.Y. Fullerton in *C. H. Spurgeon: A Biography* recounts:

> The whole Spurgeon Library, therefore, taking no count of tractates, consists of no less than 135 volumes in all, or, including the reprints, 176! If we add the albums and the pamphlets, we get an output of 200 books!

Fullerton says of Spurgeon's personal library: "At the time of his death there were 12,000 volumes in Mr. Spurgeon's library, in addition to those that he had sent to furnish the well-filled shelves of the library at the College."

Twelve thousand volumes provided the foundation of his library but, as Fullerton indicates, Spurgeon had even more books.

Spurgeon wrote, read, reviewed, distributed, and treasured books. Fullerton asserts, "To listen to his talk on books one would think that he had done nothing but read in the library all his life, and to mark his publications would fancy that he had done nothing but write."

Yet we know that Spurgeon did much more than read and write. He was a pastor; he was an itinerant preacher, he led numerous institutions, and his services were constantly in demand.

We can distill down from Spurgeon's reading habits several helps that we can employ.

1. FIND GOOD BOOKS.

In Spurgeon's library there were many used books that he found in the catalogs of second-hand bookstores. Whether used or new, find good books. Especially find hardback books that will last through the years and can be passed on to your children.

2. READ GOOD BOOKS.

Books look beautiful lined across oak shelves. However, books are meant to be read. Spurgeon exhorted: "Give yourself unto reading. The man who never reads will never be read; he who never quotes will never be quoted. He who will not use the thoughts of other men's brains, proves that he has no brains of his own."

3. READ A VARIETY OF BOOKS.

It is assumed that you will regularly feast on the Bible. Beyond that, read history, biography, hymns, classics, and good fiction. Spurgeon asserted:

> We are quite persuaded that the very best way for you to be spending your leisure time, is to be either reading or praying. You may get much instruction from books which afterwards you may use as a true weapon in your Lord and Master's service. Paul cries, 'Bring the books' — join in the cry.

4. READ AS MUCH AS YOU CAN.

Spurgeon was a uniquely gifted man. You are not Spurgeon, but it is likely you can read more books than you are presently reading. Start somewhere. Attempt two pages per day. In a month you will have read 60 pages and in three months you will finish your book. Start somewhere and then grow in your reading.

12

How do I follow a long-tenured pastor?

Following a pastor who has run well is only a problem for those who lack the character or the stamina to do the same.

BY HERSHAEL YORK

Following a pastor who has run well and gone the distance is only a problem for those who lack the character or the stamina to do the same. Taking the baton of leadership from someone who has served the church for 20 years or more is certainly not without daunting challenges and discouraging obstacles, but the advantages of stability — even when "stability" has morphed into apparent intransigence — are usually preferable to following a rapid succession of pastors who did not stay long enough to lead the people in any meaningful sense of the word.

In 1990 at only 30 years old I was called to be the third pastor of the Ashland Avenue Baptist Church in Lexington, Kentucky. My two predecessors had served for 50 and 23 years respectively. One of them, Clarence Walker, was legendary. Both Jerry Falwell and W.A. Criswell told me about his impact on their lives. My immediate predecessor, Ross Range, was the quintessential pastor, a dignified and refined man who mowed his yard wearing a tie.

The church I now serve, Buck Run, has a very different history, one marked by a long succession of very short pastorates with one notable exception: my immediate predecessor, Bob Jackson. He served the church twice for a total of two decades (his last tenure was 13 years), and under his expert leadership the church exploded with growth and grace, morphing from a sleepy rural church on the banks of the Elkhorn Creek to one of Kentucky's most vibrant and missional congregations.

He led Buck Run to found the Romanian American Mission, which today has planted over 400 churches and continues to impact Europe. His emphasis on prayer and evangelism led Thom Rainer to include a chapter called "The Miracle Called Buck Run" in his book on church growth, *Eating the Elephant*. When Jackson resigned, many members grieved his departure, even years later.

I am acquainted with the ups and downs, the blessings and not-so-blessings (curses is too strong a word!) of following long-tenured legendary pastors. While I have benefited from the stability and unity that it brings, I have faced the monolithic intransigence it fosters as well. Here's what I have learned.

TWO GREAT CHALLENGES

1. You aren't him.

Furthermore, you are never going to be him. You don't have his abilities, convictions, wisdom, skills — you can simply fill in the blank here. In fact, church members will do this for you. I lost count of how many times someone looked me in the eye with no intent to hurt or discourage but flatly stated something like, "Now I think you're really good at _____ , but when it comes to _____ , you're no (Clarence Walker, Ross Range, Bob Jackson)."

Everything in a man wants to defend himself at this point, to point out one's own strengths and value added, but the best move is simply and humbly to *plead guilty*. "I *aspire* to be as great a pastor as my predecessor. He certainly sets the bar very high. Would you commit to pray for me that the Lord might, for his glory, make me the best shepherd that I can be to his flock? I desperately want to be."

If the goal were to be more loved or revered than the previous pastor, one might have a tough and trying tenure, but the objective is faithfulness, and that lies completely in one's own control. I do not have to be revered, applauded, or appreciated to be faithful. I simply have to submit to God's will. The example of my predecessor, even the humiliation of constant reminders that I am not him, motivate me to cast myself on Christ and beg the Holy Spirit to help me be faithful.

2. Preferences become convictions.

The longer a pastor stays and does things a particular way, the less congregations distinguish between biblical mandates and pastoral quirks. Consequently, some members will be prepared to defend the practice to the death when a new pastor suggests an alternative. Children's ministries, worship styles, Sunday School practices, altar calls, and even the way the offering is received might become sources of tension and division he will encounter.

Since longevity and faithfulness were the source of the last pastor's credibility, any new pastor would be naïve to think he can make significant changes without enough time to establish them. Some problems — even some people — must be outlived or outlasted. No pastor gets a shortcut to character or credibility because they are forged in the furnace of life and experience.

TWO GREAT BENEFITS

1. Stability means predictability.

Long-tenured pastorates *usually* indicate a stable church family. A pastor typically does not have new crises that threaten his position arise after about 10 years. Through the years of his ministry those who opposed him left or changed, and every new member came in at least partly because they resonated with him. The effect is that over the course of years, the congregation coalesces behind the pastor's leadership and enjoys great unity.

While a new pastor certainly will feel the pressure of change and even of possibly disappointing all those people, he also has a church with established patterns and habits that make them predictable.

Whatever challenges follow a long and successful tenure, they aren't as bad as those presented by the church that cycled through 10 pastors in 20 years. Those churches grow accustomed to instability. They typically place far more trust in key lay leaders than in any pastor because so many pastors come and go while a key leader or two seem constant and dependable.

That kind of congregation may even see those lay leaders as their protectors from pastoral overreach and vicissitudes.

While one can always find exceptions, the general result is that the steadiness of a church accustomed to a long pastorate is easier to lead than the instability of one that has cycled through multiple short tenures. In the strength and consistency of the former, a pastor will at least get the opportunity to build bonds and relationships in a congregation that knows what long-term commitment looks like.

2. They know how to overlook faults.

Like any lasting committed relationship, the bonds between a pastor and a congregation work best when they love one another across their differences and disappointments. Frankly, the necessary skill is even more stark than that. People in happy relationships that endure acquire the ability not even to notice one another's faults. Pastors will find that true in church life as in marriage, otherwise, no pastor could last long because all men have great flaws.

Following a pastor who stayed at a church a long time means, at the very least, that this church learned how to follow a man in spite of himself and his weaknesses. Greater still, they may have learned to love him so much that they didn't notice or dwell on his flaws. If they have done that for one man of God, perhaps they can learn to do it for another.

TWO GREAT MOVES
1. Never criticize your predecessor.

If he went insane one night and slaughtered a local herd of goats with a machete, you brag on his ability to sharpen a blade. That may be an overstatement, but the point of the hyperbole is to drive home a hard and fast rule: just don't criticize him at all. Find the good things that you can say about him and say those things even if they are small. Do not be fooled by the church members who feel comfortable criticizing him to you. They will still think you petty and insecure if you join in. Just don't do it. Ever. You gain nothing and lose a great deal.

Even if a predecessor did much worthy of criticism, anyone who follows him should leave that to the Lord and others to judge. No successive pastor ever had to suffer criticism because he was not critical enough. A man with a lengthy tenure did enough right things that he survived all the business meetings, crises, funerals, deacon elections, and church splits for a long time. Do not discount that. Even if his tenure ended in shame and sin, speak only of your commitment to purity and transparency, but never in contrast to him. Everyone either already knows the truth about him, thus you need not say it, or they believe him to be better than he is, and you only anger and frustrate them when you say it.

If you are blessed to follow a man who was faithful and honorable and whose service ended well, then thank God for him, honor him, bless him, and speak well of him openly and often. I have been blessed to follow men of character and distinction in my pastorates, and I have taken every opportunity to praise them sincerely, thank God for them, and invite them back for special occasions. Even after the death of Jackson, when we dedicated our new campus 13 years after he left, I publicly thanked God for him and made sure that his widow and family were present to receive our gratitude and honor and to witness the continuing fruit of his ministry. Honoring my predecessors has never taken anything from my leadership. To the contrary, it has added value and leadership currency.

The people who were loyal to my predecessors did not see me as an interloper trying to deprive their beloved pastor of his legacy,

57

but as a fellow admirer and a grateful servant happy to build on the great foundation that they laid. They easily and quickly gave me that same loyalty and respect because I gave them permission to keep loving the man who had shepherded their hearts faithfully. I learned long ago that people have a great capacity to love and I don't even have to be their favorite pastor so long as I am a *faithful* pastor.

2. Stay a long time and be faithful.

Every time I had someone give me the "you're no Bob Jackson" speech, I knew that if I would just be faithful to love the people, preach the Word, and point people to Christ, the day would come in which someone looks at my successor and says, "You know, you're a good guy, and we like you, but you're no Hershael York."

In all candor, I take no solace that anyone might ever be compared unfavorably to me, but I understand human nature well enough to know that will happen if I am a faithful shepherd who walks through life with the precious people God has entrusted to my care. After a few years of preaching the Word, loving the people, and shepherding hearts, I have earned trust and leadership collateral, and, I pray, so will my successor. So I end where I began: Following a pastor who has run well and gone the distance is only a problem for those who lack the character or the stamina to do the same.

13

How do you shepherd a dying and divided church?

A pastor should first come in, love them where they are, earn their trust, then break the news to them of their current state.

BY JEFF ROBINSON AND BRIAN CROFT

I n his 13 years as senior pastor of Auburndale Baptist Church in Louisville, Brian Croft has seen it all. He has experienced profound lows in the ministry but has sought to remain faithful and has also seen God bring the church from death to life.

He chronicles that incredible tribute to God's grace in a new book *Biblical Church Revitalization: Solutions for Dying & Divided Churches* (Christian Focus). He founded Practical Shepherding and serves as senior fellow for the Mathena Center for Church Revitalization at SBTS. In this interview, we discuss the book and lessons learned from many years in pastoral ministry.

In the new book, you tell the story of Auburndale and relate many wise lessons learned during your time at Auburndale. When most guys enter pastoral ministry, not too many of them think of their church as dying, divided, or declining. When and how did you know you were in a revitalization situation?

I took a church with 30 elderly folks, no money, and an old but beautiful building falling down around us. The church had been in decline for over 30 years, and no pastor since 1972 had stayed longer than four years. The community around us despised the church. It was pretty obvious it was in trouble and on its last leg.

When you are in a revitalizing situation, how do you communicate that to the people in under your care? Do you ever use that language with them or speak publicly of the need to get healthy as a church?

Churches need to know they are broken and dying before real, important change can take place. Many churches do not know how bad the situation has gotten. It is a mistake for a new pastor to just come in and tell them this, although it might be true. A pastor should first come in, love them where they are, earn their trust, then break the news to them of their current state.

What's the one piece of advice you would give to a student with a newly minted degree from Southern Seminary who is about to take his first pastorate?

I would first remind them that "newly-minted degree" shows they were well trained theologically, but it did not make them a pastor. Their instincts should now be to preach faithfully and to sacrificially love and shepherd their people the first few years. Don't go if you are not willing to stay at that church five years.

What's the worst mistake you've ever made as a pastor and what did you learn from it?

That's hard to say. Many to choose from. I would say there were numerous occasions where I dismissed words of counsel from elderly members early in my ministry who proved to be right years later. I missed good opportunities to grow as a young pastor if I would have listened to them. A close second is putting people in leadership positions before they were ready.

Better than most I've ever heard, your story demonstrates the difficulty and danger of pastoral ministry. Do you think most men really think it's going to be tough when they are entering their first pastorate?

No. I think young pastors are way too idealistic about what being a pastor will be like. I partially blame the celebrity pastor culture combined with a lack of local churches taking responsibility to expose young men to the dirty, messy, daily grind that is real pastoral ministry.

How can a man go to a church and stay 10, 20, 30 years? Is that even possible or advisable in today's here-today-gone-tomorrow church culture?

Not only do I think it is possible, but those willing to do it in this type of culture you describe will show to be noble examples of faithfulness that will be rare in decades to come. I believe those willing to plant and stay will bear fruit in ways others who leave every three or four years in a church will not experience. Lasting change in a church will not come inside 5 to 10 years.

You oversee the Mathena Center for Church Revitalization at Southern Seminary. What is the main purpose of the Mathena Center and how are you integrating your own work at Practical Shepherding into that?

It is the kind providence of God that Southern asked me to play this role because it feeds so well from both my pastoral ministry in my local church and Practical Shepherding. The Mathena Center exists to help struggling and dying churches find new life and to train young men who are willing to go into these churches and engage in this hard, but noble, work. The resources of Practical Shepherding are largely used to help train these men for this work of shepherding these wounded sheep in these churches and to minister God's Word in such a way that the Spirit breathes life back into them.

14

The conviction to lead: Winston Churchill's courageous legacy

Born in the splendor of Blenheim Palace on Nov. 30, 1874, Churchill's life would span the post decisive years of the transition into the modern world.

BY R. ALBERT MOHLER JR.

Sir Winston Churchill is widely regarded as the greatest leader of the 20th century. Born in the splendor of Blenheim Palace on Nov. 30, 1874, Churchill's life would span the most decisive years of the transition into the modern world. Though faced with great adversity — and driven by a titanic self-confidence — he would emerge as the man who saved England from collapse in its darkest hour. And as Paul Johnson notes in his excellent biography, Churchill's life was large in every way.

In his 90 years, Churchill had spent 55 years as a member of Parliament, 31 years as a minister, and nearly nine years as prime minister. He had been present at or fought in 15 battles and had been awarded 14 campaign medals, some with multiple clasps. He had been a prominent figure in the first World War, and a dominant one in the second. He had published nearly 10 million words, more than most professional writers in their lifetime, and painted over 500 canvases, more than most professional painters. He had reconstructed a stately home and created a splendid garden with its three lakes, which he had caused to be dug himself. He had built a cottage and a garden wall. He was a fellow of the Royal Society, an elder brother of Trinity House, a lord warden of the Cinque Ports, a royal academician, a university chancellor, a Nobel Prizeman, a knight of the Garter, and a member of the Order of the Companions of Honour and the Order of Merit. Scores of towns made him an honorary citizen, dozens of universities awarded him honorary degrees, and 13 countries gave him medals. He hunted big game and won a score of races. How many bottles of champagne he consumed is not recorded, but it may be close to 20,000. He had a large and much-loved family, and countless friends.

Churchill's significance extends beyond his political victories and historical influence. I have argued for many years that Churchill represents a model of compelling leadership, even for Christians. In fact, it was this very point that first drew me to Churchill. When I first began to think about leadership as a teenager, I recognized immediately how much Churchill had to teach me — he was a leader of world-changing courage. When he spoke, a nation was given the hope and determination to fight a war that simply had to be won — against odds that left even many of his own friends and family convinced that England's future was already lost.

My personal fascination with Churchill has continued even into today. In my personal library, I have two entire sections devoted to Churchill's own works and books about him. In my book on leadership, *The Conviction to Lead*, Churchill is a regularly recurring figure — an exemplar of many of the virtues I think make for compelling leadership. In this article, I want to highlight some of the ways Churchill modeled effective leadership, particularly in the face of opposition.

CONVICTIONAL LEADERSHIP DEMANDS
COURAGEOUS TRUTH-TELLING

Christian leaders must always remember that leaders are speakers. Leadership requires bold, convictional, and clear communication. Churchill knew this principle and we would do well to learn from his example. In the throes of World War II, Churchill rallied the British people with his powerful and bold public addresses. As Edward Murrow explained, Churchill did not just lead a nation by sending troops to the war, he also "mobilized the English language and sent it into battle." Churchill himself recognized the remarkable effect of his words and the power they had on the nation. In one of his more humble moments, Churchill suggested the British people themselves had the heart of a lion — "I had the luck to be called upon to give the roar."

But it wasn't merely Churchill's commitment to powerful communication that made him a great leader, it was also his commitment to telling the truth even if it was unpopular or invariably bad news. William Manchester once described the difference Winston Churchill made as Britain's Prime Minister when he led the nation at the point of its greatest peril. Churchill, said Manchester, "could tell his followers the worst, hurling it to them like great hunks of bleeding meat." Of course, this did not mean Churchill was crude or cruel, but that he simply told people the truth. Churchill recognized truth alone could rally the British people in the face of danger and opposition. Churchill told them the truth about their peril, and then he told them the truth about themselves, giving Britons "heroic visions of what they were and might become." How much more should ministers of the gospel recognize the truth, indeed God's truth, is the only thing that can transform our congregations, equip the saints for the work of the ministry, and steel our spines for the battle against the world, the flesh, and the devil? Truth-telling is central to leadership. And, of course, Christians also recognize that truth-telling is not just central to leadership but central for growing in the grace of God and in our public witness for Christ.

One of the most compelling lessons we can learn from Churchill is his convictional leadership even in the face of opposition. This is something ministers of the gospel need to learn and learn well. Gospel-centered ministry will always come at a cost and will always face opposition. Jesus himself promised us "in this world you will have trouble" (John 16:33).

Churchill may now be recognized as one of the 20th century's most courageous leaders, but that was not always the estimation of his contemporaries. In fact, at the beginning of the 1930s, Churchill found himself on the periphery of power, and most had written him off as a prospect for future leadership. Because he had twice switched parties, he was not trusted within the conservative party, and he was increasingly isolated.

During this time, Churchill warned of Hitler's militarism and the rearmament of Germany, but the British political class considered Churchill to be a warmonger, not Hitler. Churchill wrote articles and gave countless speeches documenting Hitler's growing menace and his military ambitions. He so irritated Britain's prime minister, Stanley Baldwin, that Baldwin attempted to subvert Churchill within his own local constituency, just to remove Churchill and his voice from the House of Commons.

Yet when Hitler invaded Poland, the credibility of almost all of the British elite was shattered. Only one man had the credibility to lead Britain as it faced its greatest challenge in centuries, and that was Churchill. And of course the only reason Churchill maintained his credibility is because he was willing to speak the truth and warn of coming danger, even while suffering isolation and resentment from those within his own party.

Christians can learn a great deal about leadership from Churchill, particularly in the face of opposition and great danger. Churchill reminds us that leadership is impossible without true conviction. Christian leaders must recognize the stakes are even higher for us than they were for Churchill. The church is waging war against the gates of hell, and we are fighting for the souls of men and women across every nation and people group. Trials, suffering, and challenges are assured as we are faithful in this task. But true leadership demands commitment to truth, even in the face of the most hostile opposition.

15

Three ways lateral leadership develops (and proves) your leadership

If a leader fails to lead self, the leader lacks credibility to lead others and does not have much to offer. Much has been written, and aptly so, about leading oneself.

BY ERIC GEIGER

W hen people speak, write, or think about leadership, they often are thinking about "downward leadership" and influencing people they oversee. "Upward leadership," or effectively communicating to and fostering a great relationship with one's leader, is just as critical and has crushed many talented leaders. Much more challenging than both "downward" and "upward" leadership is "self" leadership. Plato wisely stated, "The first and best victory is to conquer self."

If a leader fails to lead self, the leader lacks credibility to lead others and does not have much to offer. Much has been written, and aptly so, about leading oneself.

In my opinion, lateral leadership is the least discussed leadership direction.

By lateral leadership I am referring to leading your peers. You serve alongside them but don't report to them, and they don't report to you either. Lateral leadership may be one of the most challenging aspects of leadership because it is not always clear who is responsible for the decision, who should initiate, or who should take the lead. Lateral leadership is always more art than science.

Lateral leadership both develops and proves your leadership in the following leadership disciplines:

1. COMMUNICATION

When leading laterally, you must excel in communicating with others. You must listen well, develop rapport and trust, and communicate clearly. Leaders must provide clarity of direction and expectation, and this is especially challenging in lateral leadership because competing priorities and expectations often exist. It takes a savvy and gifted leader to communicate for clarity when the reporting lines are blurry. By learning how to communicate well laterally, a leader is simultaneously trained in communicating to leaders and those the leader oversees.

2. PREPARATION

When leading laterally, you must be prepared. Unlike those on your team who have already agreed to listen to you or follow your lead, those you influence laterally are constantly evaluating how your contribution helps the overall mission and their particular area. A leader can (though a leader never should) afford to be more lax in preparation for people under the leader's supervision. This is never the case in lateral leadership. You have to bring your A-game or you take major steps backward in trust with your peers. Lateral leadership forces preparation, which both develops and proves your commitment to prepare.

3. IMPLEMENTATION

Because multiple teams are involved, implementation is most likely to "fall through the cracks" in lateral leadership. Wise teams declare a point-person, but because the point-person does not have formal authority outside the project, it takes a strong leader to implement when hard lines of authority do not exist, which is one big reason lateral leadership prepares you for other leadership environments. If you can implement well without formal authority, you prove you do not need a title to get something done.

Lateral leadership, though often challenging, develops leaders in communication, preparation, and implementation. If you are seeking to be developed as a leader, look for opportunities to lead laterally.

This article originally appeared at ericgieger.com. Used with permission.

16

Nine Sources of conflict in congregations

Today's pastor can be overwhelmed with the demands of leading a congregation, especially during an age of information overload.

BY LARRY PURCELL

W hen I left the military over 30 years ago to pursue my calling to be a pastor, I naively believed my training in conflict resolution would not be necessary. I found out quickly that this was not true. Today's pastor can be overwhelmed with the demands of leading a congregation, and especially during an age of information overload. Conflict and change are partners, and the speed of change is closely connected to the influences of transportation and technology. The speed at which we move and communicate affects all our daily decisions. I recall the time I could get in my car for private moments of reflection and prayer when driving to visit a church member in the hospital. Then a pastor may be expected to drive to a hospital if it is a critical situation.

Today's pastor could have just returned from visiting someone in the hospital, receive a call on his smart phone and return to the hospital the same day. H.B. London writes about the demands placed upon a pastor today in *Pastors at Greater Risk*. London states in the opening chapter about several shifts in moral, social, and economic conditions that are battering congregations. Conflict may not be on the pastor's agenda, but it does occur with or without warning. James said whenever you experience various trials, not *if* you may experience trials (James 1:2).

This chapter will explore some sources of conflict in congregations. Some are identified by Roy Pneuman and the Alban Institute, and are conflicts I have personally experienced as a pastor. The purpose of this chapter will be to identify in what ways these sources of conflict may have application in a church during an era of rapid social and cultural changes.

PEOPLE DISAGREE ABOUT VALUES AND BELIEFS

We can define values in various ways across cultures and regions. A wise leader will ask questions and listen to what a congregation says it values and then look to see if what they are doing matches what they say. I've heard church leaders say they value a ministry such as reaching young adults. I can see what a congregation values by how they spend their money and how they spend their time. When asked to consult with a church, I will look at documents such as church budget, latest finance statements, calendar, and how they staff for ministry. Such critical documents will best describe what is valued by a church and its leadership by how they invest their resources. I challenge you to examine what you say you value and then study your personal calendar and bank account.

Churches are people not buildings. A congregation can deviate from its mission by being busy about what may seem important for the moment. An issue can be important but not the mission the Lord intended for a church. Skilled leaders must assess carefully what their church values as most important early upon his arrival. As a wise counselor, you are listening carefully to what they state is important. You compare this to what they have in church documents. A pastor should be making an assessment as to how a church compares to what God's Word demands as most important. The Apostle Paul declares what is most important to the mission of the people of God, the gospel (1 Cor. 15:3-5). A question I will ask as I review a church's documents and ministries is, "Where is the gospel in this ministry or activity?"

A CHURCH'S STRUCTURES ARE UNCLEAR

Structural ambiguity about two critical issues, authority and accountability, can create conflict. Authority is the ability of a leader to make decisions. If a leader has the authority to make decisions, to whom are they accountable? I have been the pastor of a church that stated it desired me to lead and make changes. I would attempt to lead a change and find that not all the congregation would agree with me having this authority. My research across the state of Kentucky would survey pastors and congregational leaders perceived expectations of a pastor. I found a great disparity between not only pastors and lay leaders, but also between lay persons serving as deacons and those serving on search teams. In many Southern Baptist churches, the search team can be seen as the hiring team, but in most churches the deacons are leaders a pastor will work with most closely. If lines of authority and accountability are not clearly defined the new ministry leader may experience conflict.

Clearly defined lines of authority and autonomy are critical as a church or a ministry experience significant growth. Growth is desired by churches, but growth can only be sustained if adjustments are made to issues of decision making.

PASTOR'S ROLES AND RESPONSIBILITIES

A new pastor is often encouraged to lead changes; however, it may be the changes desired by a group in the church. The last section dealt with clear boundaries with accountability and authority. If a new ministry leader does not have clearly defined roles and responsibilities he or she may rely upon what they did at the last church or ministry position. If you are a new pastor, you should spend quality time asking groups in the church to see what they see your roles and responsibilities to be. This may sound redundant since you just experienced this with a search team. This can be a reality test for a new leader. You are seeking to discover how younger and older members, married and single adults, perceive the position of ministry leader. It is also quality time listening to the membership. You most often hear what you expect, but the critical point is you are seeking their input. They first want to know you care for them as a new leader, and you demonstrate this by asking and listening. A wise leader will start to lead changes with the areas of agreement between the membership and the leader. You can probably see that the nursery needs new toys and carpet. When you talk with the nursery workers and hear this, then you can move changes and reduce conflict. You are more critically building essential relationships with your membership.

The new pastor or ministry leader needs to have guidelines and expectations that best fit the church's expectations and needs. The pastor's roles and responsibilities must be developed to be helpful and responsive to the pastor's level of skill. Churches usually have a one-size-fits-all when developing a job description of the pastor or a ministry leader description.

STRUCTURE NO LONGER FITS THE SIZE OF A CONGREGATION

Traditional or established churches tend to see themselves as they did in the past. A church will often seek to call someone to lead the church in growth. The resistance will come when some of the church members value competing changes. Insanity has been stated as wanting to do the same things the same way but coming up with different result. For a church to be healthy she must regularly re-evaluate her dreams and processes.

A church I was pastor of continued to see herself as a large church. Its systems were defined as multi-staff and large budget. What challenged this was the church had a time of conflict reducing the membership from over 1,000 persons attending worship to only 200. The immediate challenge for me was to use data to demonstrate to the trusted leadership that critical adjustments must be made to the budget and staffing. This change in how the membership viewed itself must be biblical and not just for the sake of growth. I challenged the leadership and members to re-organize around the gospel. I see 1 Corinthians 14:40-15:8 as a challenge in a time of confusion as moving toward what is most important. The Apostle Paul said in 15:3 "most important" and then proceeded to describe the gospel. The correct question during the time is not if something is good or comfortable. The question to guide in reducing conflict is: "Where is the gospel in every activity and ministry?"

I am going to offer the following guide as a church seeks adjusting its structures and processes.

Chapel church. This is usually a church below 100. The numbers used in this section are only arbitrary. It is critical to the life of the chapel church to have either one person or family who holds the keys to all decisions. They are critical insuring the church's doors are unlocked, building maintained, and decisions are made. This church seeks a minister to serve in the role of chaplain. A chaplain-pastor will teach and preach, oversee funerals and weddings, and pastoral care. The chaplain-pastor must build critical relationships with the trusted key-holder(s) before recommending any change in reducing chances of conflict. What is critical for the new pastor to grasp is that he must excel at the work of a chaplain before he can be seen as pastor. A common expression by the members at this stage is referring the pastor as preacher. The name pastor follows building trusted relationships by being a good shepherd of the membership.

Pastoral church. A church must have a strong pastor to break the 100 barrier. The chapel church has one person who influences most of the decisions. If a pastor can establish trusted relationships with critical decision makers in the church, the keys can be handed to him. Strong pastoral leadership is seen by the one who builds critical relationships, visiting members, offering insights into changes that will benefit the church, and sharing the gospel in the community. This type of leader can be a calming presence because of the strength of leadership is demonstrated.

Ministry-driven church. A critical number for the strong pastoral leader to know is 150. As the church grows in attendance, a pastor can only minister effectively to no more than 150 persons. When a church has grown beyond the 150 number in its largest service, usually Sunday morning worship, there is a diminishing return. Churches may experience some tension when this level of growth occurs. Members have enjoyed close personal contact from the lead pastor that to invite another staff member or lay leader to do hospital visits, is resisted. It becomes critical for the lead pastor to see his role of building the ministries of a church as the means to reach the lost and disciple to redeemed. *True biblical leadership is not just getting things done, but helping persons know Christ and grow in Christ (evangelism and discipleship).* Ministries are driven by a church's context and the gifts/passions of the membership. A ministry-driven model in an urban context will be drastically different from one in a rural context. As the pastor witnesses the growth of a ministry, he must enlist help for its sustained growth, and as a means of equipping and empowering the congregation (Eph 4:12).

Team-driven model. This church model will see significant growth and health in one or more ministry areas. The numbers are not meant to be exact, but this model is most effective in a church with attendance nearing or exceeding 300. I have witnessed growth in churches that came mostly from its student and children's ministries. This growth also resulted in greater needs for discipleship and small groups for the entire membership. When a church experiences growth in students and children's areas the church has a responsibility to minister to the entire family.

A warning with the team-driven model. It is not uncommon for a church to both support and resist this model. Member's see the need for the model when it is explained to them, but they may resist because they may be used to and relish the personal attention of the lead pastor. Team models take a lead pastor who is willing to hear comments such as, "I thought this was the pastor's job?" or "What is the pastor doing now?" It is critical for the lead pastor during this stage to develop a team approach to ministry. When the youth minister or other ministry team leaders have a successful event, be sure you recognize those leading the work. It undermines the team-driven model to take credit for the success of others in the ministry. A team leader is willing to take all the blame for failures, and to give the credit of successes to others. A team-driven model must not be seen as handing off your work to others. Rather, team ministry is an effective way to enlist and equip believers to use his or her gifts for the kingdom of our Lord (Eph 4:12).

Board-led model. The larger a church grows the more complex the issues of authority and accountability become. Clear lines of communication are critical to accomplishing the mission of the church, so as a church grows it will be challenged to reorganize itself. *A healthy church will seek to reorganize herself often to ensure she is accomplishing the Great Commission and great commandment.* It is critical that as the context of a church changes so will how it reaches the lost, disciples the saved, and connects to its community. The definition of a larger church can be arbitrary and can have several variables. The gifts and desires of the pastor and pastoral team, and the gifts and desires of the congregation will impact the direction of the administrative processes. Scripture provides examples of how the early church handled issues of crisis as in Acts 6 with the widows and the Jerusalem council of Acts 15. While Acts 6 describes a process, it does not prescribe a set of processes for all churches in the ages to come. Thus to be a New Testament church does not require have seven deacons. The critical factor in Acts 6 was that the Apostles were not to be distracted from the Word and prayer. In Acts 15 there is a disagreement, but it is a doctrinal issue, and the solution of how the Gentiles are to be accepted is prescriptive for all churches. The challenge of the larger church is organizing in a way to have the proper balance of accountability and authority in decision making. Often a group of leaders are selected from among the congregation. Examples of this are found in Exodus 18 when Moses became overwhelmed with doing the work alone. Additionally, we find in 1 Timothy 3 and Titus 1:5-9, New Testament illustrations of godly leaders selected to serve in critical church roles. Decentralized power is what this is often called in secular terms. It is used in business and military, but I believe it originated in scripture. The nations around Moses had a king making all decisions. The Lord was teaching Moses through the words of Jethro to empower a group of godly leaders to come along beside him in the work. The Apostle Paul would be facing his death as he wrote to Timothy and Titus. The work of the Lord must continue and 2 Timothy 2:2 was the method to meet this demand, *commit to faithful men who will be able to teach others also.*

The shifts in church structures move a pastor and ministry teams to an Ephesians 4:12 ministry of equipping and empowering leaders. When a pastor is entrusted with the power to lead, he must distribute this decision-making power to ministry team leaders. Shifting from a pastor-led church to ministry-led and then team-led leadership requires credibility and trust with the membership. These shifts in administrative processes build greater lay involvement in ministry (leadership as a discipleship model). Board-led models are designed to provide the proper amount of decision making power to the pastors and ministry teams, while maintaining the proper balance of accountability.

NEW PASTOR RUSHES INTO CHANGES.

I am often asked; how often should a new pastor seek to make changes? The statement I share is: To the degree that the congregation perceives a crisis, they will empower the leader to initiate certain changes. If the key members of a congregation see the need for a change, the pastor can lead the changes, but if they don't see it then it is dangerous to rush into a new initiative. An effective pastor will spend quality time getting to know his people and hearing their heart. This valuable time in conversation with the people will also assist a leader in understanding when they are ready to make changes. If the nursery is in shambles, often the families with younger children see it as well as the workers in the nursery. An effective leader is less interested in who gets the credit than accomplishing the work of the Lord. The wise pastor/leader will encourage changes as often as possible through trusted lay leaders. The leaders greater task is to build a sense of urgency to move a change forward.

COMMUNICATION IS BLOCKED.

A pastor and congregation must have both vertical and horizontal lines of open communication. Vertical lines of communication between a congregation and the Lord are developed through worship, the Word, and prayer. Horizontal lines of communication are between persons and are developed as we love one another. A healthy church will grow in membership and/or ministries. Growth creates challenges for all levels of leadership to have open lines of vertical and horizontal communication.

CHURCH PEOPLE MANAGE CONFLICT POORLY.

A pastor or church consultant, I have witnessed many pastors and church leaders avoid conflict at all cost. When talking with church leaders too many see all conflict as evil. Since the Fall of Humanity, we have experienced broken communication vertically and horizontally. Sin continues to hinder our ability to relate to one another. In the death, burial, and resurrection of Jesus the Messiah we have our hope (1 Cor 15). When I read 2 Corinthians 5, I am reminded that we needed to be reconciled to God and it is Jesus who provided this reconciliation. Reconciliation itself speaks of someone who is in conflict with another. All humanity was in conflict with God and one another. God reconciled everything to Himself through Christ (2 Cor 5:18, 19). We now have peace with our Lord through the grace of Christ. All believers are sent forth as ministers of reconciliation because He has committed the ministry of reconciliation to us. Pastors should never be shocked when encountering conflict in a congregation.

Roy Pneuman provided these insights into church conflict:

- Conflict is inevitable.
- Conflict is a part of life.
- Conflict creates the energy that makes change possible.
- Conflict becomes destructive if it is mismanaged.

James 1:2 tells the believer to *consider it a great joy, my brothers, whenever you experience various trials.* The word for joy is also the word used for grace in the Bible. It is in the crucible of conflict that pastors and lay leaders develop spiritual insights and tenacity. During times of greater trials inside our being or in our contexts, we build greater communication and dependence upon our Lord. A proper theology of conflict is critical to effective ministry.

Concluding this chapter is difficult because so much more needs to be said about church conflict.

A leader's personality is critical because many pastors are training their head and not their heart. The desire for quick results demanded by many church members puts the pastor in a challenging position. How fast should changes be initiated by a new pastor? When is a church ready for new changes? Leadership is both art and science. The science of leadership can be learned from books. The art of leadership is lived by understanding the context and loving the people. Dependence upon the Holy Spirit is essential to the life of any pastor and the success of the Lord's work. All the leadership skills available to a minister are useless unless the God the Spirit provides the power. It is conflict that the Lord has used in my life to humble me in the work and to seek greater dependence upon him. The pastors devotion and spiritual disciplines must increase as he faces conflict.

17

Two lies every pastor's wife needs to stop believing

The Lord would demolish my idea of the perfect pastor's wife over the next few years, mainly through my own sin and my husband's long-suffering.

BY NIKKI DANIEL

O n January 7, 2006, I dove into the trenches of ministry doe-eyed and unsure of myself. Although I began attending church services when I was about 12 years old, I had never seen the behind-the-scenes of ministry. So, when the Lord brought a handsome pastor into my life, I had no idea what to do. I certainly wasn't an ideal pastor's wife (you know the kind: soft-spoken, sweet in all situations, never critical, perfect wife and mother, even more perfect Christian).

The Lord would demolish my idea of the perfect pastor's wife over the next few years, mainly through my own sin and my husband's long-suffering.

The years 2006 through 2008 would be filled with irate church members, somber theological conflict, and a revolving church membership door.

When I got the call about speaking at the Sojourn Network Leader's Summit earlier this year, I immediately began jotting down notes. The topic would be "The Pastor's Wife and the Dumb Things We Do." Within 60 seconds, I had eight mistakes that I had made in my nearly 11 years of being a pastor's wife. I was able to narrow it down to two mistakes so that I could keep in the given time frame (but I could have easily gone longer!). The first mistake was assuming that the behind-the-scenes of ministry would be free of hardship. The second was underestimating the importance of having deep friendships both inside and outside of the local church.

ILLUSION 1: MINISTRY WILL BE FREE OF HARDSHIP

I unwittingly believed that pastor's wives had it all together. On top of that, I thought, "Hey, we're all Christians here, right? We're all seeking to honor the Lord and love each other. Surely ministry is going to be easy."

If ministry was going to be easy, then having it all together would be just as painless. I thought my role would simply be to pray with other women, disciple younger girls, and maybe lead a Bible study all with a Holy Spirit smile on my face.

However, I quickly realized that ministry was difficult and that it wasn't about the appearance of perfection. When church members yelled at my husband during a member's meeting, I didn't have it all together. I actually left the meeting in angry tears. When our congregation dwindled down to 25 people, I didn't have it all together. I doubted the Lord's calling for this particular church body. When other churches called to see if my husband was interested in switching pastorates, I didn't have it all together. Giving way to my fear, I nagged my husband to take a different pastorate.

The reality of my own desperation for the Lord squelched the appearance of perfection. And boy, was I desperate. Ministry was full of hardship and I had to trust that the Lord was leading my husband, who was in turn leading me. The trenches of ministry were unsettling. I prayed for my husband to have strength, and

I prayed that I would be able to point him to the Lord on the hardest of days. Over time, the hardship of ministry was no longer terrifying. It actually became sweet because it was, as Spurgeon so beautifully put it, the wave that threw me against the rock of ages.

Ministry was hard and I didn't have it all together. But those two weaknesses gave way to the incredible strength of the Lord. I became a pastor's wife who was completely desperate for the strength of God thanks to his sovereign goodness in the hardships of ministry.

My husband never wavered in his commitment to the local body here in Augusta. He believed that the Lord was working the hardships for good. Now, 11 years later, the church is unified and thriving. This didn't come about because things were easy or because we were an impeccable power couple ready to take on the church. It came about because the church was not dependent on us. It was dependent on the kind and loving hand that created it.

ILLUSION 2: HAVING DEEP FRIENDSHIPS BOTH INSIDE AND OUTSIDE THE LOCAL CHURCH IS UNIMPORTANT

Not only was ministry more difficult than I anticipated, but friendships were more complicated than I realized. While engaged, I met with a seasoned pastor's wife who gave me advice on various aspects ministry. Her biggest emphasis was on friendships. "Do not get too close to women in the church. I've been burned and my family has suffered because I made that mistake." Because I was doe-eyed and had unrealistic expectations, I brushed her off as a bitter woman who didn't know how to love well.

I dove immediately into friendships within the church, which did end up biting me during those difficult first few years. One of my mentors was someone in the aforementioned situation who yelled at my husband in a member's meeting. It was disheartening and incredibly discouraging. While I can see the temptation to throw off all deep friendships within the church, I simply couldn't see a good argument for it in Scripture. In fact, I felt that the women in our local body were intentionally placed in my life for accountability, love, and friendship. These are women with whom I linked arms to spread the gospel message. We sang praises to our Lord hand-in-hand. We cried together, fasted together, and walked through difficult times together. How could deep friendships not form in these situations?

I also saw much wisdom in investing in friendships outside of the local church body. There are certain situations about which I need advice that are best discussed outside of my church friends. There is also something to be said for having friends who don't know your local church body and the ins and outs of your church. My encouragement for pastors' wives is to find two to three really good friends inside the church and two to three really good friends outside of the church. This has proven to be an enjoyable and spiritually beneficial balance for me.

I'm confident that I will continue making mistakes as a pastor's wife until the day I die. However, there is great comfort in knowing that while I am on this rocky road of sanctification, the perfect and holy God reigns supreme over any and all hardships and friendships in life. He provides his strength through my weaknesses, which far outweighs any pastor's-wife-concocted perfection or friendship scheme that I can devise.

Ministry wives, you're going to make mistakes. You'll do dumb things sometimes. You may struggle through the hardships of ministry or be burned by a friend in the church, but know that the Lord is using these situations for good. Don't be afraid to be a desperate-for-Jesus ministry wife. Those are the best kind anyway.

This article was originally published on the Sojourn Network's blog.

18

Why credibility matters more than anything in Christian leadership

Leadership matters! It matters in the home. It matters in the workplace. It matters on athletic teams and in musical groups. And, of course, leadership matters in the church.

BY JUAN R. SANCHEZ

L eadership is such an important issue that there is no end to the writing, selling, and buying of leadership books. In fact, we can even say that this blog is about leadership — helping pastors grow in their leadership of the church. But how should we assess leaders — both present leaders and future leaders? Unfortunately, we (and our churches) assess leaders based on competency and results. Can he "preach"? Is the church "growing"?

Now, before we get into what I'm about to say on leadership, let me offer a disclaimer: I am NO leadership expert (whatever that may be). However, I have made lots of mistakes from which the Lord has taught me much. Regardless, my thoughts on leadership are not dependent on having enrolled in "the school of pastoral hard knocks." Instead, my thoughts are dependent on what Scripture itself says about church leadership. And according to Scripture, there are more important qualities to assess in leaders than "competency" and "results." Allow me to offer, then, some biblical thoughts on leadership assessment and development.

As we assess and evaluate leaders in the church (both present and potential leaders), consider these four "C"s of biblical leadership:

1. **Character:** Whereas we tend to elevate competency as the highest qualification for leadership, the Bible highlights character: men of godly character, as outlined in 1 Timothy 3:1-14 and Titus 1:5-16. The basis character quality of a godly man is above reproach. To be above reproach means that when (not if) accusations come against an pastor, they do not stick because he is not characterized by what he is being accused of. Paul shares four areas in which an elder must be above reproach:

- **Above reproach in his character:** The pastor, though not expected to be perfect, must be a man who pursues holiness and is characterized by fighting sin: "sober-minded, self-controlled, respectable, hospitable, ... not a drunkard, not violent but gentle, not quarrelsome, not a lover of money (1 Tim 3:2-3).

- **Above reproach in his family life:** The pastor must be a man who has first displayed maturity in shepherding his own household well. He must be faithful to his wife, not neglecting her but loving her and caring for her; he must be faithful in his parenting, disciplining his children. If someone cannot manage his own house, how will he be able to manage God's house (1 Tim 3:4-5)?

- **Above reproach in his public life:** The pastor must also be well thought of by outsiders (1 Tim 3:7). How will a pastor lead if he does not have a good reputation?

2. **Conviction:** A pastor must also be a man of biblical

convictions and above reproach in his doctrinal life. He must be a mature and maturing believer (not a new convert). "He must hold firm to the trustworthy word as taught, so that he may be able to give instruction in sound doctrine and also to rebuke those who contradict it" (Titus 1:9).

3. Care: The word "pastor" indicates feeding, protecting, caring for a flock. Pastors or elders, then, are called to "shepherd the flock of God that is among you" with love and compassion, leading by example (1 Pet 5:1-4). Some evidences that men care for the flock are — they are with the flock when we gather on the Lord's day; they are with the church when it publicly cares for one another in members meetings; they care by displaying deeds of love for other members (prayer for members, visitation of the sick or shut in, practicing hospitality with other church members); they care for other brothers by engaging in discipling relationships; and they care for unbelievers by sharing the gospel regularly.

4. Competent: While Scripture emphasizes character over competency, the pastor must be a man who is "able to teach" (1 Tim 3:2). He must be able to not only teach God's people God's word; he must also be able to refute opponents of the gospel with kindness and patience so that the Lord may grant even these gospel enemies repentance (2 Tim 2:24-26).

These four "C"s observed over time (1 Tim 5:22) produce credibility. At High Pointe, we utilize the following leadership formula when observing men for the office of pastor (elder):

C (character) + C (conviction) + C (care) +
C (competency) = Credibility
T (time)

Again, I am no leadership expert, but Scripture is clear — we should consider men for office who are above reproach and who love the church enough to care and protect the flock, feeding it with God's word. As pastors, let's strive to be such men, and let's look to raise up such men in our churches. As we focus on faithfulness as leaders, we are freed to trust the Lord for whatever results he sees fit to bless us with.

Resources

RECOMMENDED LEADERSHIP READING FROM R. ALBERT MOHLER JR.

The Conviction to Lead: 25 Principles for Leadership That Matters
R. Albert Mohler Jr.

The God Who Goes before You: A Biblical and Theological Vision for Leadership
Timothy Paul Jones and Michael S. Wilder

Good to Great
Jim Collins

The Leadership Challenge
Kouzes and Posner

Leadership
James MacGregor Burns

Classic Drucker: From the Pages of Harvard Business Review
Peter Drucker

The Effective Executive
Peter Drucker

On Becoming a Leader
Warren Bennis

Why Should Anyone Be Led by You?
Rob Goffee, Gareth Jones

The Leaders We Need: And What Makes Us Follow, Michael Maccoby
Transforming Leadership
Leighton Ford

Getting Things Done
David Allen

Executive Presence
Harrison Monarth

Leadership: Essential Selections on Power, Authority, and Influence
Barbara Kellerman

92

Contributors

Scott Connell is executive pastor of worship at First Baptist Church, Jacksonville, Florida, and assistant professor of music and worship leadership at Boyce College.

Brian Croft is senior pastor of Auburndale Baptist Church in Louisville, Kentucky, and is the founder of Practical Shepherding, Inc. He is also senior fellow for the Mathena Center for Church Revitalization and an adjunct professor at The Southern Baptist Theological Seminary. He is the author of several books including *The Pastor's Ministry* and *Biblical Church Revitalization*. He is the husband of Cara and father of four children.

Nikki Daniel is a pastor's wife from Augusta, Georgia. Nikki and her husband, Bert, have two sons and one daughter. She enjoys homeschooling, writing, and playing intense games of Settlers of Catan. Nikki holds a MATS degree from Southern Seminary.

Eric Geiger is senior vice president at LifeWay Christian Resources and leads the organization's resources division. He has a doctorate in leadership and church ministry from Southern Seminary and is the author or co-author of several books, including *Creature of the Word* and *Simple Church*.

Matthew Hall was appointed dean of Boyce College in 2016 and also serves as senior vice president of academic strategy at Southern Seminary. He also serves as assistant professor of church history.

Timothy Paul Jones is C. Edwin Gheens Professor of Christian Family Ministry, associate vice president for the Global Campus, and pastor at Sojourn Midtown. Jones has authored or contributed to more than a dozen books, including *PROOF, Conspiracies and* the Cross, Perspectives on Family Ministry, and Christian History Made Easy. He is married to Rayann and they have three daughters.

R. Albert Mohler Jr. serves as president of The Southern Baptist Theological Seminary and as the Joseph Emerson Brown Professor of Christian Theology. In addition to his presidential duties, Mohler hosts two programs: "The Briefing," a daily analysis of news and events from a Christian worldview; and "Thinking in Public," a series of conversations with the day's leading thinkers. He is the author of several books, including He Is Not Silent, The Conviction to Lead, and We Cannot Be Silent. He is married to Mary, and they have two grown children.

Larry Purcell is a regional consultant for the Kentucky Baptist Convention. Previously, he has served as professor of church leadership and associate dean of advanced degree administration.

Thom S. Rainer is president and CEO of LifeWay Christian Resources. Rainer received both a M.Div. and Ph.D. from Southern Seminary and was founding dean of the Billy Graham School of Missions and Evangelism from 1994 to 2005.

Jeremy Rhoden is the co-owner of Louisville Overstock Warehouse and serves as a trustee at Southern Seminary. Jeremy lives with his wife, Catherine, in Louisville, Kentucky, where he is an elder at Clifton Baptist Church.

Ray Rhodes Jr. is president of Nourished in the Word Ministries and pastor of Grace Community Church of North Georgia. He is the author of Family Worship for the Christmas Season, Family Worship for the Thanksgiving Season, Family Worship for the Reformation Season, The Marriage Bed, and The Visionary Marriage, along with numerous articles on marriage and the family. He is presently writing a new biography on Susannah Spurgeon, which will be published by Moody Press.

Jeff Robinson is editor of *Southern Equip*, pastor of Christ Fellowship Church in Louisville, senior editor for The Gospel Coalition, adjunct professor of church history at Southern, and senior research and teaching associate for the Andrew Fuller Center. He is co-author with Michael A. G. Haykin of *To the Ends of the Earth: Calvin's Missional Vision and Legacy* and co-editor with D. A. Carson of *Coming Home: Essays on the New Heaven and New Earth*. Jeff and his wife, Lisa, have four children.

Juan R. Sanchez is assistant professor of Christian theology at Southern Seminary and is president of the Southern Baptists of Texas Convention. Since 2005, Sanchez has served as senior pastor of the High Pointe Baptist Church in Austin, Texas. In addition to training pastors in the United States, Latin America, South America, and Eastern Europe, he is also a council member of The Gospel Coalition and co-founder and president of Coalición por el Evangelio.

M. David Sills, A.P. and Faye Stone Professor of Christian Missions and Cultural Anthropology, is the founder and president of *Reaching & Teaching International Ministries*, a missions professor at The Southern Baptist Theological Seminary, speaker, and author. His latest book is *Hearts, Heads, and Hands: A Manual for Teaching Others to Teach Others* (B&H, 2016).

Randy L. Stinson is senior vice president for academic administration, Basil Manly Jr. Professor of Leadership and Family Ministry, and Provost at Southern Seminary. A recognized authority on the subject of biblical manhood and womanhood, Stinson is a regular conference speaker on the subjects of parenting, marriage, and men's leadership. He is the co-author of *A Guide to Biblical Manhood* and co-editor of *Trained in the Fear of God: Family Ministry in Theological, Historical, and Practical Perspective*.

Michael S. Wilder is J.M. Frost Associate Professor of Leadership and Discipleship (2006) and associate vice president for doctoral studies at Southern Seminary. Wilder's ministry experience includes serving as a youth pastor for 12 years in Georgia and as a pastor for three years in Kentucky. He taught for New Orleans Baptist Theological Seminary on the adjunct faculty for three years prior to moving to Kentucky. In addition to his ministry at Southern Seminary, Wilder serves as senior pastor of First Southern Baptist Church, Floyds Knobs, Indiana.

Hershael W. York serves as Victor and Louise Lester Professor of Christian Preaching at Southern Seminary. He is also senior pastor at Buck Run Baptist Church in Frankfort, Kentucky. He is the co-author of *Preaching with Bold Assurance*. He is married to Tanya and they have two grown sons.

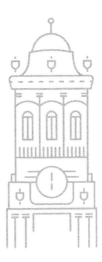

Ministry leaders choose Southern

Whatever your calling, The Southern Baptist Theological Seminary will train you to serve faithfully in your ministry context. In preaching, missions, counseling, shepherding, and teaching, Southern Seminary prepares ministry leaders for more faithful service. Did you know Southern offers multiple programs aimed at leadership?

 DEGREES OFFERED

- M.A. in Church Leadership
- M.A. in Theological Studies
  (Lay Leadership)
- M.Div. in Leadership

- D.Min. and D.Ed. Min in
  Executive Leadership
- D.Min. and D.Ed. Min
  in Leadership

Explore those and more at **sbts.edu**.

THE SOUTHERN BAPTIST
THEOLOGICAL SEMINARY

SOUTHERN
EQUIP

A growing collection of resources for
the growing challenges of ministry

FIND THESE RESOURCES AND MORE AT *EQUIP.SBTS.EDU*

**How to care
about social
justice (with-
out losing
the gospel)**

Russell Moore

**He's
memorized
42 books of
the Bible, and
you can too**

Don Whitney

**Faith that
moves
mountains:
what Jesus
didn't mean**

Tom Schreiner